The Book of the Silver Ghost

The Book of the
SILVER GHOST

Including a complete facsimile of
an original Silver Ghost Instruction Book

With an introductory essay by KENNETH ULLYETT

Motorbooks International
Publishers & Wholesalers Inc.
Osceola, Wisconsin 54020, USA

Originally published by Max Parrish and Company Limited, London. Reprinted by permission of the original copyright holders by Motorbooks International Publishers & Wholesalers, Inc., Osceola, Wisconsin 54020, USA. All rights reserved, no part of this publication may be reproduced without prior written permission from Motorbooks International. Printed and bound in the United States of America.

Library of Congress Cataloging in Publication Data
Main entry under title:

The Book of the Silver Ghost.

Reprint of the ed. published by M. Parrish, London.
1. Rolls-Royce automobile. I. Ullyett, Kenneth.
TL215.R6B66   1977   629.22'22   77-23149
ISBN 0-87938-041-1

Introduction

UNDOUBTEDLY somewhere in Samarkand, on the higher slopes of Popocatepetl or along the banks of the Limpopo, there is someone to whom Rolls-Royce is a name without magic . . . someone who does not know the story of how Frederick Henry Royce, engineer, met the Hon. Charles Rolls, twenty-seven-year-old man-about-town with a passion for ballooning . . . someone who has indeed never even heard the fascinating story of the Silver Ghost which was born out of their meeting and which is universally recognized as the most fabulous luxury car of all time.

For just such an ignoramus (but not, of course, for you, as no doubt you are already thumbing through the illustrations) the next few pages are written; and those who have heard it all before may perhaps be induced to regard this text with a tolerant nostalgia, as a well-emulated ritual.

Sir Henry Royce, surely one of Britain's greatest engineers, was born just over 100 years ago on 27th March, 1863, in the village of Alwalton, near Peterborough. He was the fifth child of James and Mary Royce, both from milling families, and they moved to London when Henry was four. Five years later, the father died, leaving the family penniless.

The boy had an extremely hard upbringing, and during those five years in London he had only one year of schooling. He sold newspapers at W. H. Smith's bookstalls at Clapham Junction and Bishopsgate Station, became a telegraph boy at a Mayfair post office, and his mother worked as a housekeeper. When he was fourteen, an aunt managed to raise the £20 a year premium to enable him to enter the Great Northern Railway locomotive works at Peterborough as an apprentice, under the charge of Mr Frederick Rouse. One of his first jobs was to help convert the historic Stirling 'eight-foot' coupled 4 – 4 – 0's into single-wheelers.

'Fred – we always called him Fred – was one who worked on that job,' recalled an old-time craftsman named Yarrow, at whose house Royce lodged, 'and in course of time he began to make himself quite a good mechanic, though I wouldn't say he was over-quick at the mastery of tools. Once, I recall, he and I and another mechanic were sent out to rescue a broken-down loco, and it was through some of Fred's suggestions we got her back many hours later. . . .'

At nights and at weekends Royce learned more engineering in the little workshop which was Yarrow's garden shed. He read, caught up on lost years of schooling. This ended suddenly within three years, when the aunt could no longer afford the £20 annual premium, and he was forced to find another job. A

Leeds firm of machine-tool makers, whose chief output at that time was for the Italian Arsenal, paid him eleven shillings a week for fifty-four hours, often from 6 a.m. until 10 p.m. This was Victorian England.

Then back to London for a while and a job with a pioneer electric power company which had bought certain Hiram Maxim patents rivalling those of Edison. Royce lodged in Kentish Town, read books on this new-fangled electricity, attended Professor Ayrton's night-school and the Polytechnic, and at length felt entitled to call himself not only engineer but electrician. As electrician he got a job with the Lancashire Maxim and Western Electric Company in Liverpool, in which city Royce was installing street-lighting before he was twenty years of age. However, within two years the parent company in London went into liquidation, and once more Royce was looking for work.

With a friend Ernest Claremont he decided to set up on his own as an electrical engineer. He had £20 capital. Claremont had £50. With this they took a small workshop in Cook Street, Manchester, producing electric fittings, bells, dynamos. Within ten years the little concern of F. H. Royce & Co. became a £30,000 public company, with £9000-worth of orders on the books. They were very good electric fittings, bells and dynamos. A growing part of the business was also concerned with excellent electric cranes which Royce designed, and the great demand for Royce dynamos for cotton mills, ships and other lighting plants brought prosperity. Royce and Claremont were now Members both of the 'Mechanicals' and of the Institution of Electrical Engineers, and Royce was an acknowledged expert on commutation, lamp-filament construction and the three-wire system for public power services.

He married, in 1893, the charming daughter of a London professional man, Alfred Punt, built a pretty house at Knutsford, Cheshire, and planned a tidy garden. Everything about Royce had to be tidy, even the shrubs and trees, and, like other prosperous men of the age, he took up the new hobby of automobilism. His first car was a Decauville. His second car – a Royce. Three of these experimental cars were built to his own design, and became the despair of his fellow directors of Messrs Royce Limited who already had major worries as the effects of the Boer War were now hitting Manchester industry. It was distressing that the engineering head of the Company should be careering around the dusty roads of Cheshire in an autocar, spending late night hours perfecting a 'combustion engine' instead of designing new electrical machinery to combat the growing cut-price competition of Germany and America.

Three sets of castings and other parts were ordered for the experimental Royce car, the first of which – with Royce at the wheel – took the road on the auspicious day of 1st April, 1904. The second car was handed to Ernest Claremont, and the third a few months later became the property of one of the leading automobile distributors in London, the Hon. Charles Stewart Rolls, son of Baron Llangattock and pioneer motorist and aviator.

Young Rolls was probably one of the most fearless and expert drivers among the handful of British pioneers at the turn of the century. However, he was no mere dare-devil. His technical knowledge was considerable. He left Cambridge with a degree in Mechanics and Applied Science. Apart from his pioneer ballooning, he was soon winning laurels in motor-racing. In 1900, in a 12 h.p. Panhard, Charles Rolls won the Thousand Miles Reliability Trial promoted by

Lord Northcliffe. Three years later he established a world land speed record at Phoenix Park, Dublin, at the wheel of an 80 h.p. Mors.

His partner in the firm of C.S.Rolls & Co., motor agents, was Claude Goodman Johnson who had already made a great reputation in the motoring world as the founder-secretary of the Automobile Club later to become the Royal Automobile Club. Johnson and Rolls dealt in Panhard, Whitlock-Aster, Mors, Gnome and a few other petrol automobiles (all of them foreign-built, except the New Orleans, constructed not in New Orleans, U.S.A., but in Twickenham, Middlesex, although basically the Belgian Vivinus), as well as the Gardner-Serpollet steamer. They had a West End showroom in Brook Street, Mayfair, and a repair shop ('A separate lock-up compartment is provided for each car undergoing repair') in the former Lillie Hall skating rink, Seagrave Road, Fulham. Here C.S.Rolls & Co. were official repairers to the War Office and the Royal Automobile Club.

Their customers included Captain the Hon. Guy Ward, motor pioneers including Worby Beaumont and most of the landed aristocracy of Edwardian England. Their articled pupils, incidentally, at various times included Captain Owens, Lord and T.O.M.Sopwith. In their horseless carriages Rolls's wealthy customers wanted opulence and comfort; they also wanted reliability such as few Continental cars could provide.

At this juncture a Mr Henry Edmunds who was a minor shareholder in one of Claremont's companies, and who as a committee member of the R.A.C. was also a friend of Rolls, was loaned one of the experimental Royce 10s. He was so impressed that in the spring of 1904 he wrote: *My dear Rolls – I have pleasure in enclosing you photographs and specification of the Royce car, which I think you will agree with me looks very promising. . . . The people have worked out their designs in their own office, and knowing as I do the skill of Mr Royce as a practical mechanical engineer, I feel sure one is very safe in taking up any work his firm may produce. . . .*

Royce and Rolls, at first both too busy to meet, eventually agreed to Henry Edmunds acting as 'umpire' at discussions, and later he revealed: 'I well remember the conversation I had in the dining-car of the train with Mr Rolls, who said it was his ambition to have a motor-car connected with his name so that in the future it might be a household word, just as much as "Broadwood" or "Steinway" in connection with pianos, or "Chubb" in connection with safes. . . . I remember we went to the Great Central Hotel at Manchester and lunched together. I think both men took to each other at first sight. . . .'

Rolls was loaned one of the 10s, drove it to London and in characteristic enthusiasm woke up Claude Johnson in the middle of the night to let him see how beautifully it ran. Next day an agreement was signed appointing C.S.Rolls & Co. as sole distributors, and on 23rd December, 1904, Royce Ltd contracted to supply C.S.Rolls & Co. with four different types of chassis ranging from a two-cylinder 10 at £395 to a 30 h.p. 6 at £890, this latter being the forerunner of the Silver Ghost in many respects. Subsequently Rolls discarded the sale of other makes, and became united with Royce under the name of Rolls-Royce Ltd, with Claude Johnson as managing director. Capital was not easy to raise, and an incident concerned with a vital cheque for £10,000 is detailed in the caption to Plate 27 (page 19).

Success came with almost every car Royce designed. The 10, exhibited at the Paris Salon in 1904, was awarded a special medal and diploma by the commissioners. Rolls-Royce 20s were entered for the 1905 Tourist Trophy Race. Rolls himself, driving No. 1, stripped his gears and had to retire, but Percy Northey, driving the second 20, No. 22, took second place to an Arrol-Johnson driven by its designer John Napier. Full advantage was taken of the lessons learned by the car's first public appearance, and the following year a Rolls-Royce 20 won the T.T. by the handsome margin of twenty-eight minutes over the car which gained second place. The four-cylinder T.T. car broke the Monte Carlo-to-London record in May, 1906. The new 30 h.p. 6 won the battle of the cylinders in the same year in competition with a foreign four-cylinder car, being the only six-cylinder car out of seven entries to complete the tough route of the Scottish Reliability Trials, completing 671·5 miles non-stop.

At Claude Johnson's insistence, the Company began a one-car policy, based on the 48 h.p. six-cylinder chassis which Royce developed during the late summer of 1906. This was a 6 composed of twin blocks each of three cylinders (the 30 h.p. 6 had three blocks of two cylinders), with a 'square' engine of 4½-in. bore and stroke. The dual magneto and coil ignition of the 30 was retained and improved; the same type of four-speed gearbox with overdrive top (direct drive on third) was used.

'Anything appertaining to automobile mechanism,' said *The Autocar* of 15th December, 1906, 'which issues from the works at Manchester under the direction of that finished and talented engineer Mr Royce, is certain to attract the immediate attention of the motoring world. Therefore a few points dealing with the new 40/50 h.p. six-cylinder Rolls-Royce engine which made its first bow to the world at Olympia are certain to interest our readers. . . .'

The writer praised the water-jacketing, the single camshaft, the interchangeable inlet and exhaust valves of nickel steel, the generous bearing proportions, valve actuation through roller-ended rocking levers to minimize tappet wear, and, of course, the novel method of engine suspension in the frame.

The distinguished Rolls-Royce historian Mr C.W. Morton, to whom I am indebted for so much of the information given here (as indeed must be all others who write about the make), has set the facts in what I am positive is the correct order regarding that common misconception as to how the 40/50 came to be known as the Silver Ghost.

The first Rolls-Royce car to have an individual name was the 20 (chassis No. 24263) sold to Captain the Hon. Guy Ward. Claude Johnson dubbed it 'Grey Ghost', commissioned a guild of arts and crafts to design a nameplate in repoussé style. Other wealthy automobilists taking delivery of special to-order Rolls-Royce adopted names like 'Scarlet Pimpernel', 'Cookie' and 'Beauty Gal'. However, Grey Ghost seemed most appropriate to a Rolls-Royce and, says Mr Morton: 'This association of a car with silent motion seemed to start a trend, for the next car to follow this pattern was the thirteenth 40/50 h.p. six-cylinder made in 1907. This was named Silver Ghost. Many external metal parts of this car were silver-plated, and the coachwork was finished in aluminium paint.

'These had, up to this time, been given to individual cars, but Silver Ghost gained great distinction, and among other achievements beat the world's non-stop record in 1907 with an R.A.C.-observed run of 15,000 miles. This basic type remained unchanged until 1925. The original Silver Ghost is now in the Company's ownership and is still an active performer after covering over 500,000 miles. It was decided to bestow this as a type-name to all succeeding 40/50 chassis of this design.'

In the whole nineteen-year run of the Silver Ghost, there were only two exceptions. Two 40/50s were entered by CJ for the 1908 combined 2000-mile International and Scottish six-day trial. As no premium was placed upon silence in this event, the B.H.P. was increased to 70 by raising the compression-ratio. CJ had named these cars White Ghost and Silver Silence, but on hearing them had the names changed to White Knave and Silver Rogue. In that same year a 40/50 exported to India won the Bombay–Kolhapur Trial and secured the Mysore Cup. This car was nick-named Pearl of the East, chassis No. 60576, thirty-seventh of the 40/50s to be produced. It had a port-able-top limousine body by Cockshoot of Manchester.

'It was later acquired by the Maharajah of Gwalior,' I was told by Mr Morton, 'and without a doubt made a tremendous impression on the many Indian rulers and princes who were very motor-minded. . . .' The Nizam of Hyderabad (then the richest man in the world) ordered a Ghost (chassis No. 2117) in 1913 on which a richly ornamented throne was mounted in place of the normal rear seats. H.R.H. the Maharajah of Patiala had at one period a stud of twenty-two Rolls-Royce cars including a Ghost with solid silver fittings.

In such ways the Ghost was becoming the epitome of refinement. A contemporary catalogue states: 'The man who goes to Poole's for his clothes, Purdy for his guns and Hardy for his rods, goes to Rolls-Royce for his car.' The car was becoming a symbol, almost a legend. And at Manchester and the new Derby Works (officially opened by Lord Montagu of Beaulieu on Thursday, 9th July, 1908) there were deities and

minor deities among the men who designed and built Ghosts. Royce, of course, was R. Rolls was CSR. Claude Johnson, CJ. Others included Hs (Ernest Walter Hives, later to become first Baron Hives), Rg (engine designer A. J. Rowledge), Ep (Eric Platford) and W (Arthur Wormald, a tool-maker who came to R from Westinghouse, and who became works manager and a director of Rolls-Royce Ltd).

Hs, who had joined the Company in 1908, drove the special model of the Ghost which CJ entered for an R.A.C.-observed test of a top-gear, non-stop London–Edinburgh run designed to beat the claims of the rival Napier. One of their 65-h.p. cars had already made this run on a top gear of 2·7 to 1, showing a fuel consump-tion of 19·35 m.p.g., and with over 76·4 m.p.h. reached on a concluding timed speed test at Brooklands. With Hs at the wheel, the 40/50 made the run on a 2·9 to 1 top gear, gave a fuel consumption of 24·32 m.p.g. and did the timed speed run at 78·26 m.p.h., thus beating the Napier's performance all round.

Sporty élite in the Charles Rolls circle had been unable to buy either the one-off White Knave or Silver Rogue, but R, CSR and CJ agreed there was no reason why the 'London–Edinburgh', with its special coach-work and minor modifications, should not be available to the general public. It was listed in the current catalogue as 'Rolls-Royce touring car, London to Edinburgh type', at £1154 15s. for the chassis (plus £65 for C.A.V. electric lighting, £15 15s. for Elliott speedometer, £15 12s. 6d. for Beatonson glass screen) with 'four grooved Dunlop tyres and body to seat four'.

The car which originated this type was chassis No. 1701 E, and an expert on the model, Dr R. O. Barnard, says: 'Its body was the narrowest possible that could be made to cover the full width of the chassis frame. . . .

A shallow projection on the right side of the scuttle was presumably made to permit the driver's foot to use the throttle pedal. From the scuttle the bonnet tapers to a low radiator, presumably the 20-in. type which was standard at that time. The striking difference between this car and other contemporary Ghosts was the provision of cantilever rear springs sliding in trunnions attached to the under-surface of the back-axle casing. This arrangement was the distinguishing feature of the early L-to-E-type cars, for at that time the standard 40/50 had three-quarter-elliptic springs. L-to-E-type cars with chassis numbers higher than 1994 mounted their cantilever springs over instead of under the axle, as did all Silver Ghosts from chassis 2100 onward. . . .'

A slightly larger carburetter was fitted, and the compression-ratio was raised by omitting packing beneath the blocks. These minor changes increased the B.H.P. of the L-to-Es by some 15 per cent at 2000 r.p.m. Long after the event of September, 1911, coachbuilders such as Barker, Cann and Midland Counties Garage were providing Ghosts with L-to-E-type coachwork on sporting lines, and in 1913 a unique Victoria phaeton of L-to-E type was supplied to special order for the Duke of Sutherland.

'In 1913,' says Mr Morton, 'four 40/50-h.p. Rolls cars, entered in the Great Austrian Alpine Trials and driven by Hs, Friese, "Jock" Sinclair and James Radley, beat the cream of Continental cars and drivers in epic fashion. It was intended to call this model the Continental, but the name which captivated the public fancy and finally stuck was Alpine Eagle.' Several of these cars, including Radley's 1913 Alpine, are still preserved, immaculate in appearance, and Mr Stanley E. Sears' Alpine (Plate 13) is typical.

The London-to-Edinburgh type and the Alpine Eagles were primarily sports Ghosts, and silence was not their main virtue. However, that hoary old cliché perpetuated by many motoring writers overawed by their first test of a Rolls-Royce (example, '*The loudest sound I heard at 60 m.p.h. was the ticking of the clock*') is much older than generally supposed. Said *The Autocar* on 27th April, 1907:

'At whatever speed this car is being driven on its direct third, there is NO engine so far as sensation goes, nor are one's auditory nerves troubled driving or standing by a fuller sound that emanates from an eight-day clock. There is no realization of driving propulsion; the feeling as the passenger sits either at front or back of the vehicle is one of being wafted through the landscape. . . .'

Because of minor changes through the years (for example, the stroke increased to 4·75 in. for the 1910 models, moving the ignition and carburetter controls from dash to steering column in 1911, the London-to-Edinburgh modifications, and introduction of the four-speed box in 1913) there is in fact no complete record at Derby of all Silver Ghost chassis numbers. In the spring of 1959 that indefatigable honorary secretary of the Rolls-Royce Section of the Vintage Sports-Car Club, Mr S. J. Skinner, compiled a first list, amended at the end of that year by Mr Michael Vivian, honorary Registrar of Cars of the 20-Ghost Club. The upshot of their conjoint investigations appears to be as follows: From 1907 to 1913 chassis numbers were numerical, with the prefix '60' for the earlier cars. For some unexplained reason, R did not issue 600 or 800 series. *1907*, 60539 to 60592. *1907–8*, 60700 to 60799. *1908–9*, 919 to 1015. *1912*, 1800 to 1899. *1913*, 2200 to 2699 (Ghosts bearing chassis numbers 2704E, 2709, 2720 and so on exist, although officially there is no record of a 2700 series). *1913–14*, CA 1–20, NA 1–59,

MA 1–56. *1914*, AB 1–67, GB 1–49, EB 1–60, PB 1–65, LB 1–68, YB 1–66, RB 1–68, UB 1–67. *1914–15*, BD 1–32, TB 1–37 and No. 55. *1915–16*, AD 1–32, CB 1–37, ED 1–34, PD 1–33, RD 1–35, AC 1–28. *1919*, PP 1–36. *1920*, TW 1–81, CW 1–102, FW 1–121, BW 1–165, AE 1–141, LE 1–141, RE 1–81, PE 1–81, YE 1–81, UE 1–81, GE 1–81, EE 1–41. Also War Office series WO 1–101, and to WO 279 for War Office series 1920–7. *1921*, CE 1–101, NE 1–111, AG 1–182, LG 1–198, MG 1–213, JG 1–76, UG 1–97, SG 24–91. (Mr Vivian finds that some of the AG, MG and UG series chassis have 1921–2 features.) *1921–2*, TG 1–94, KG 1–43, PG 1–44, RG 1–43, YG 2–81. Also ZG 1–81, HG 1–102, which may be 1922–3. *1923*, LK 1–100, NK 1–100, PK 1–63. *1923–4*, EM 1–135, LM 1–71, RM 1–103, AU 1–141, TM 1–103. *1924–5*, some AU series, also UE 1–126.

As mentioned in the detailed caption to Plate 22 (page 18), in 1919 CJ started a subsidiary company to produce the Ghost in the United States, at Springfield, Mass. Some of the CE, NE, LG, JG, SG, AG, MG, UG, TG, KG, MF and RL series were Springfield-built, and later a number of the New Phantoms up to the PR series.

The following plates illustrate some of the more interesting Ghosts extant. Stories of them, and of others, are legion.

When Mr Millard W. Newman, of Tampa, Florida, discovered a 1912 Ghost it was little more than a wreck. Both cylinder blocks were smashed. He wrote to the R.-R. Motor-Car Division Service Station at Hythe Road, London, for help. After a lengthy search, Hythe Road found an old Rolls-Royce instruction manual and an old pair of cylinder block castings which needed much modifying and machining. Six months (and eighteen coats of paint) later Mr Newman had his

Ghost running. Thirty-six years ago a Mrs Christie of Dorset lost her chauffeur, so her Ghost chassis was jacked up and stored. It did not come to light again until 1956, when it was sold by the executors to an American owner who had it fitted with a contemporary Brewster tourer body. However, the chassis was brand-new and unused, so on application the Company willingly issued their normal three-year-guarantee.

It is a fascinating misconception that the famous 'Lenin Rolls' seen on show in Moscow belonged in its earlier life to the last reigning Czar of Russia. In fact, the Czar's two 1913 landaulettes have returned to Britain, being purchased by Lord Furness before Russia became a Soviet Republic. The Ghost formerly owned by Lenin is a 1919 car, chassis No. 16X, exhibited at the 1920 Olympia Show, delivered to Mr Leonid Krassin, then head of the Soviet A.R.C.O.S. trade legation. In the late 1920's the Soviet authorities ordered a batch of Ghost armoured cars, similar to the W.O. series used by Lawrence of Arabia and described in his *Seven Pillars of Wisdom* (see Plate 26).

Not all such famous cars have been preserved. At the outbreak of the First World War the Company presented a Barker limousine to Lord Kitchener, then Secretary of State for War. It was in fact the car which took Kitchener to his port of embarkation when he boarded the cruiser, subsequently torpedoed, on which he lost his life. Lloyd George took Kitchener's place at the War Office, and later retained the car and its chauffeur when he became Prime Minister. Later he purchased it for his personal use, and ran it for thirty years. The Imperial War Museum had to decline the offer of this car, so all of it except the radiator, kept as a relic, went under the hammer of a scrap-metal firm.

By contrast, in the backwoods of Canada, outside Vancouver, a 1910 Ghost engine drives a sawmill, still doing a first-class job for loggers in a remote camp. Two of these Ghosts were imported in 1910 at a cost of $10,000 each, joining Stanley steamers, Franklins and high-waisted Model-T Fords on Vancouver city streets. About 1919 they were sold, one being shipped to Japan, the other broken up and, so it was thought, scrapped. Then in 1959 it came to light at Alert Bay, 180 miles north of Vancouver, a sawn-off part of the chassis still carrying a plate showing the legend: 'Rolls-Royce, London and Derby, No. 1905 E.'

Royce, made a baronet in 1930, outlived the Ghost by eight years. He died at the age of seventy, working to the last. Since CJ, second of the great triumvirate, died in April, 1926, Royce had borne the burden and carried on the splendid tradition alone. Rolls, of course, was thirty-two, in the prime of life, when he was killed in an air crash at Bournemouth on 12th July, 1910.

There are memorials to him near his home at Monmouth, and at Dover, and a memorial plaque at the Derby Works. 'But we in Rolls-Royce,' says Mr Morton, 'like to think that the finest monument to C.S.Rolls was fashioned by Rolls himself when, with Henry Royce, he founded this company in 1904 and helped to establish the traditions which have since guided it.'

If any other memorial were needed, surely it is to be found in the Silver Ghost itself, which Royce designed yet which would never have existed but for Rolls. . . .

Notes on the Plates

IN SOME instances more detailed information is given in the following list than it is possible to print, owing to reasons of artistic display, in the captions to individual plates. Unless otherwise specified, all illustrations (together with the reproduction of the Silver Ghost 'Instructions for the Care of Rolls-Royce Cars') are the copyright of Rolls-Royce Limited, and are reproduced by special permission.

Plate 1
40/50 on the Grand Tour. A scene of the 1920's, the car being on an Alpine test while R was wintering at Le Canadel, most southerly point on the French Riviera.

Plate 2 (top)
Garden discussion about the Ghost. R beneath his favourite mulberry tree in the garden of his West Wittering home, Elmstead, with (*centre*) Mr C. L. Jenner, senior designer, and (*right*) Hs, Mr E. W. (later Lord) Hives.

Plate 2 (lower)
Engineering conference. Basil S. Johnson (*second from left*), managing director after the death of his brother Claude, and (*extreme right*) engine designer Rg – A. J. Rowledge.

Plate 3 (left)
R's birthplace, Alwalton, a few miles from Peterborough. The house no longer exists, nor does the nearby mill, where R's father was once miller. *Photo: H. Bowles, Peterborough.*

Plate 3 (right)
R at Elmstead, West Wittering, the mansion previously owned by the romantic novelist Maurice Hewlett, and where *The Forest Lovers* was written. Here R is with 1 Ex, the first post-war Ghost. In the rear is an early 20, of the 40 GI series first introduced in 1922.

Plate 3 (lower)
R at his villa, La Mimosa, Le Canadel, the building of which was started in 1912 and from where, owing to ill-health, he largely directed the engineering fortunes of his company.

Plate 4
The Hon. Charles Stewart Rolls, M.A., son of Baron Llangattock and pioneer motorist and aviator. This Langfier camera study was presented to the author by CSR's sister, Lady Shelley-Rolls.

Plate 5
Claude Goodman Johnson, CJ of the Rolls-Royce triumvirate, first secretary of the Automobile Club of Great Britain (subsequently the Royal Automobile Club), for two years partner with the Hon. Charles Rolls in C.S.Rolls & Co., later to become managing director of Rolls-Royce Limited. He coined the publicity name Silver Ghost.

Plate 6 (top)
C.S.Rolls & Co.'s repair shop at Lillie Hall, Seagrave Road, Fulham, London S.W.6. This was originally a roller-skating rink, with an Italian asphalt floor.

Plate 6 (lower)
Lillie Hall, immediately prior to deliveries of the first 40/50 Ghosts. Most of the cars seen here are Heavy 20s and 1905–6 30s built at Cook Street, Manchester.

Plate 7 (top)
The Company's Ghost, AX 201, chassis number 60551, Barker-bodied tourer. First introduced in 1906–7, type in production for nineteen years. Although affectionately known as 'Old Number One', this is believed to be actually the thirteenth 40/50 manufactured.

Plate 7 (lower)
On Continental cars the ignition-control segment was engraved 'Advance' and 'Retard'. R believed this was confusing to English chauffeurs, and used the words 'Early' and 'Late' instead. This is the view from the driving position of the Company's Ghost.

Plate 8
The Company's Ghost, thirteenth in line, in a lovely English setting near its birthplace. The Hon. C.S. Rolls's personal set of silver-plated oil-lamps are mounted on the scuttle. The windscreen and Warland detachable rims are not original.

Plate 9 (left)
Dash of the Company's Ghost, 60551. Centre dial is the oil-gauge. The two circular switches below are for magneto and coil ignition systems respectively. The Elliott combined speedometer, clock and distance recorder on the right was a fifteen-guinea extra in 1907.

Plate 9 (right)
R's Duplex (two-jet) carburetter, seen on the engine of 60551. In a Scottish reliability trial this gave a consumption figure of 17·02 m.p.g.

Plate 10
Two 40/50s were entered by CJ for the R.A.C. International Touring Car Trial, 1908, provisionally named White Ghost and Silver Silence. When it was discovered the regulations included no award for silence, R was asked to have the compression-ratio increased on these two cars – and the names were appropriately changed to White Knave and Silver Rogue, the latter seen here after making fastest time on all hills including Shap Fell and Kirkstone Pass.

Plate 11
Edwardian elegance. One of the group of oil-paintings specially commissioned by Charles Rolls and CJ for the 1910 Silver Ghost catalogue. Charles Sykes, R.A., the noted sculptor, provided the paintings, and the following year accepted the commission to produce a suitable mascot for the radiator cap, 'Spirit of Ecstasy'.

Plate 12
Edwardian sporting scene, second of the group of four paintings commissioned from Charles Sykes, R.A. While this painting was being completed, Sykes was working on the first mascot 'Spirit of Ecstasy', today usually incorrectly nicknamed 'The Flying Lady', which made its appearance on Ghosts from 6th February, 1911.

Plate 13
Mr Stanley Sears' 1914 40/50 Alpine Eagle. Chassis No. 17 RB. Open four-seater by Portholme Coach Works, London. This car was sold to Captain Milburn by James Radley in 1914, and is a sister Alpine Eagle Ghost to that with which Radley won the Austrian Alpine Trial of 1914. *Photo: Stanley E. Sears and J. W. Thomas, A.R.P.S.*

Plate 14
The classic perspective cut-away drawing of the 1906 Silver Ghost engine by Max Millar, specially produced for *The Autocar* of 19th December, 1952, for which Millar himself wrote a charming essay 'A Ghost from the Past'. *Reproduction by courtesy of 'The Autocar'.*

Plate 15
A Derby Works record photograph of a Ghost engine about to be lowered into a chassis.

Plate 16
A photograph from the Silver Ghost catalogue of 1910. Engine then had 4¾-in. stroke. Pressure-feed to rear fuel tank. Three-speed gearbox, until four-speed box introduced in 1913.

Plate 17
Polished 1912 exhibition chassis. Production models of this type formed the basis of the famous Alpine Eagle which swept the board in the Austrian Alpine Trials of 1913 and 1914. New features first seen on this 1912 chassis included cantilever rear springing, four-speed box with direct drive on top, greater ground clearance and increased-capacity cooling system.

Plate 18
The year, 1910. The Ghost, a landaulet in the chassis series between 1200 and 1399, outside Tiffany's.

Plate 19
Oxford Street, London, 1910. This landaulet cost £1408 0s. 2d., with extras including speaking-tube to driver (£3 3s.), cobra bulb horn (£4 2s. 6d.) and petrol funnel (6s.). Electric C.A.V. lighting throughout (not fitted to this car) cost £65.

Plate 20 (top)
Alpine Trials, 1913. In this picture are Hs (later Lord Hives) and Eric Platford, one of the men with R from the early days in Cook Street, Hulme, Manchester.

Plate 20 (lower)
Silver Rogue, her output increased to 70 B.H.P. by lengthening stroke and increasing compression-ratio, was successful in the 1908 R.A.C. 2000-mile International Touring Car Trial. In the concluding speed trial at Brooklands, Silver Rogue averaged 53·6 m.p.h. for 200 miles on the track.

Plate 21 (top)
A few months after Silver Ghosts were being produced at the Derby Works, CSR met the Wright Brothers at

Le Mans. Wilbur Wright took him up for his first flight in a powered craft. The Wright Brothers are here seen in a 1908 Ghost.

Plate 21 (lower)
A reminiscence of the Ghost 15,000-mile trial. An authorized halt at the Cat and Fiddle Inn, at the crest of the famous hill on the edge of the Derbyshire Peak District, Buxton. The Ghost today known as the Company's Old Number One (AX 201, chassis No. 60551), with Claude Johnson at the wheel, is extreme left. CSR is at the wheel of the next Ghost, AX 205. Fifty years after this photograph was taken, in September, 1952, members of the 20-Ghost Club turned back the pages of history, re-enacted the run to the Cat and Fiddle, on the occasion of a Silver Ghost Rally to celebrate the jubilee of AX 201. *Photo: W.F.Sedgwick Ltd.*

Plate 22 (top)
In 1919 CJ started a subsidiary company to produce Rolls-Royce Ghosts in the United States. Production was started at works originally built for the American Wire Wheel Company, Inc., at Springfield, Mass., with a Canadian, Mr E.J.Belnap, as president. Production ceased in 1926, soon after the introduction of the New Phantom. A typical Springfield 40/50 is seen here.

Plate 22 (lower)
For a brief period during 1905–6 Royce produced a 30 B.H.P., 6000-c.c. six-cylinder car, chassis numbers ranging from 23927 to 60538. Fewer than fifty were produced when CJ induced the Company to concentrate on the Ghost and adopt a one-car policy which remained unchanged until the production of the 20 in 1922.

Plate 23 (top)
H.R.H. the Prince of Wales (later the Duke of Windsor), on the occasion of a royal visit to Liverpool. His Ghost tourer is followed in procession by an earlier landaulet, *circa* 1912.

Plate 23 (lower)
H.R.H. the Prince of Wales during the First World War, en route for G.H.Q. at St Omer, where he served as a staff officer and frequently took the wheel of a War Office Silver Ghost.

Plate 24 (top)
During a royal visit to Quebec in 1919, as part of the Victory celebrations after the First World War, H.R.H. the Prince of Wales used a Derby-built Ghost. Within two years many such cars were being produced at Springfield, Mass., for American and Canadian users.

Plate 24 (lower)
Of the several 40/50s owned and used by the Prince of Wales, this Salamanca cabriolet here seen at St James's Palace is one of the most attractive, and became known as a type as the 'Prince of Wales' cabriolet. *Photo: Author's collection.*

Plate 25
Victory drive at Kew, Surrey; the Prince of Wales at the wheel of his own Silver Ghost.

Plate 26 (left)
After the 408·8 m.p.h. record established by Flight-Lieutenant G.Stainforth in 1931, the Rolls-Royce 'R' engine was immediately removed (being 'time-expired' after its flying life of half an hour), and loaded on to this waiting 40/50 Phantom lorry.

Plate 26 (right)

R, who never flew, talks to some of the men who broke records with the 'R' engine. This aircraft work was initiated at Derby by Rg's (A.J. Rowledge's) team, and at West Wittering by a project design team headed by E (A.G. Elliott) and R himself. *Photo: Graphic Photo Union.*

Plate 26 (lower)

During the Gallipoli campaign in the First World War the Rolls-Royce No. 3 Squadron Car Division (commanded by Josiah Wedgwood, of the famous china manufacturing concern) was shipped to Egypt for operations against Senussi tribesmen. Later the squadron was commanded by the Duke of Westminster, and by then comprised twelve Ghosts accompanied by Model-T Ford light transports. At the end of 1916, the cars were handed over to Lawrence of Arabia. All the Rolls-Royce 'ships of the desert' were named after British men o' war, and the Ghost seen here (with a former Derby apprentice on the running-board) is 'H.M.S. Chesapeake'. *Photo: A.G. Morrall.*

Plate 27 (top)

During the First World War, Field Marshal Sir Douglas Haig (as he then was) used a Ghost for his personal transport, and a fleet of similar Ghosts was used by H.M. King George V when he visited the Western Front. *Photo: Crown Copyright.*

Plate 27 (lower)

Ghost 1776, originally carrying a landaulet body, re-bodied in 1925–6 as an ambulance for the Brighouse U.D.C. This was the fourth Rolls-Royce purchased by successful Yorkshire textile manufacturer Arthur Harry Briggs. He was known as 'The Godfather of Rolls-Royce' because soon after the introduction of the Silver Ghost, in anxious times for the motor industry, there was a risk of a Rolls-Royce public issue of £100,000-worth of shares failing. Mr Briggs immediately wrote out a cheque for £10,000, warding off the unhappy prospect of an undersubscribed share issue. He accepted a seat on the Board, and subsequently owned four Silver Ghosts.

Plate 28 (top left)

Mr Stanley Sears' 1912 Hooper limousine, chassis No. 1721. The original owner was Lord Wavertree who used the car until his death when it was stored in a barn at a Wheatley, Oxfordshire, farm where it remained for some fifteen years. In 1945 it was purchased by Mr S. E. Sears who restored it to new condition. *Photo: Stanley E. Sears and J. W. Thomas, A.R.P.S.*

Plate 28 (top right)

1911 limousine, chassis No. 1543, owned by Mr W. F. Watson, M.A., secretary of the 20-Ghost Club. Coachwork by Joseph Lawton, in 'Tulip' style. This car was supplied in 1911 to the order of Mrs S. Benger of The Grange, Knutsford, Cheshire, a near-neighbour of R during the time the earlier cars were being produced in Manchester. *Photo: W. F. Watson.*

Plate 28 (lower)

1914, London–Edinburgh type, chassis No. 27 BD, now owned by Mr Clarence Kay, California. A note in Rolls-Royce documents states: 'Received on test, 1914.

Plate 29 (top)

D. W. and M. R. Neale's Fuller enclosed-drive limousine of 1910, chassis No. 1392. Winner of the Blenheim

Palace Concours d'Élégance, 1960. *Photo: D.W. and M.R.Neale.*

Plate 29 (lower)
1912 seven-seater limousine by Barker which at £3000 reached the second highest price paid at the auction of the collection of Mr J.C.Sword, East Balgray, Ayrshire, in September, 1962. *Photo: Ulric Simson Advertising.*

Plate 30 (left)
Interior of the No. 1 shop, Derby Works, 1908. Milling machines.

Plate 30 (right)
A group of small capstan lathes in the No. 1 shop. 'Henry Royce, his health failing fast, was an incredible man,' says a former Derby executive. 'He was chief engineer and works director. He not only worked out modifications to the Silver Ghost in time for the 1907 Motor Show at Olympia, but he also designed the Derby factory himself.'

Plate 31
No. 1 Gate, Nightingale Road, Derby, 1908. In his speech at the opening ceremony of the Derby Works, CSR (then technical managing director) said: 'To produce the most perfect cars, you must have the most perfect workmen; and having got these workmen it is then our aim to educate them up so that each man in these works can do his particular work better than anyone else in the world.'

Plate 32
First non-stop transatlantic flight was made by John Alcock and Arthur Whitten Brown on 15th June, 1919, in appalling weather conditions. The two 360-h.p. Rolls-Royce Eagle engines made the Newfoundland–Ireland 1890-mile crossing in a coast-to-coast time of 15 hours 57 minutes, an average speed of 110 m.p.h. Claude Johnson gave all Silver Ghost workers a day's holiday. This photograph is taken at a subsequent window display at the Conduit Street showrooms.

'40/50' on the Grand Tour

At Sir Henry's Wittering home. (*Centre*) Mr C. L. Jenner, senior designer, and (*right*) Mr E. W. (later Lord) Hives

Engineering conference. Basil S. Johnson (*second from left*), managing director after the death of his brother Claude, and (*extreme right*) engine-designer A. J. Rowledge

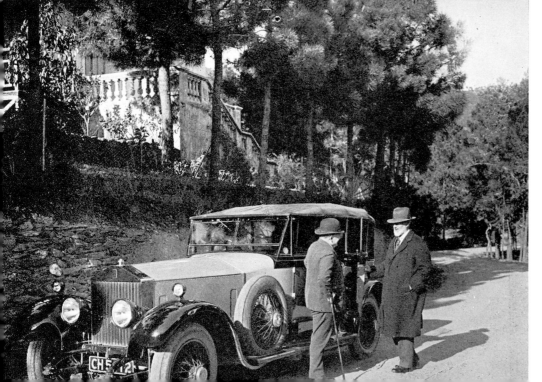

R's birthplace, Alwalton, near Peterborough (*top left*)

R, West Wittering, with 1 Ex, the first post-war Ghost. In the rear, one of the first 20's (*top right*)

R's house at Le Canadel (*bottom*)

The Honourable
Charles Rolls, M.A.

Claude Goodman Johnson

C. S. Rolls & Co's Lillie Hall repair shop (*top*)

Lillie Hall, immediately prior to deliveries of the first 40/50 Ghosts (*bottom*)

The Company's Ghost. AX 201, chassis number 60551, Barker-bodied tourer. First introduced in 1906/7, type in production for nineteen years (*top*)

On Continental cars the ignition control segment was marked 'Advance' and 'Retard'. R thought this confusing to English chauffeurs, used 'Early' and 'Late' instead (*bottom*)

The thirteenth Silver Ghost in a lovely English setting near its birthplace. The Hon. C. S. Rolls'
own silver-plated oil lamps are mounted on the scuttle

Dash of 60551. Centre dial is oil-gauge. Two circular switches are for magneto and ignition coil respectively. Elliott speedometer and clock combined, at right (*left*)

R's two-jet carburetter on the Company's Ghost. In a Scottish Reliability Trial, this gave a figure of **17·02** m.p.g. (*above*)

Silver Rogue, one of Claude Johnson's 'Heavenly Twins', in the R.A.C. 2000 miles Trial, 1908

Edwardian elegance. One of the group of oil paintings by Charles Sykes, sculptor of the Rolls-Royce mascot 'Spirit of Ecstasy'

Edwardian sporting scene, 1910. This painting, also by Sykes, does not show the mascot,
which was not produced until the following year

Mr Stanley Sears' 1914 40/50 Alpine Eagle. Chassis no. 17 RB. Sister car to that with which James Radley won the Austrian Alpine Trial

Max Millar's classic perspective cut-away drawing of the 1906 Silver Ghost engine

Ghost engine photographed at Derby, ready for installation in chassis

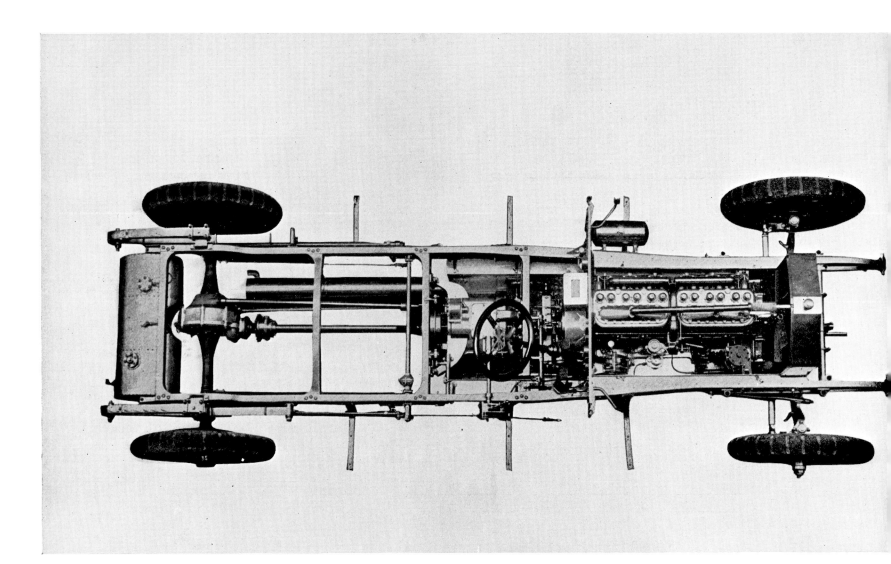

Chassis plan, 1910 Ghost

Show chassis, 1912, during which year chassis numbers ranged from 1800 to 1999

1910, Rolls-Royce becomes internationally known

Oxford Street, Maison Lewis. Rolls-Royce. The height of fashion in 1910

Alpine Trials, 1913. In the picture, Hs (later Lord Hives) and Eric Platford, one of the men with R from the beginning

Silver Rogue, 70 h.p., 1908 International Touring Car Trial

1909, C. S. Rolls with the Wright Brothers (*left*)

'Cat and Fiddle', Buxton, halt during the 1907 R.A.C. 15,000-mile Rolls-Royce Trial

Springfield 40/50

30 h.p. forerunner of the Ghost

Ghost follows the Prince, on the occasion of the visit of the Duke of Windsor (then Prince of Wales) to Liverpool

H.R.H. the Prince of Wales en route for G.H.Q. at St Omer

1919, H.R.H. the
Prince of Wales visits
Quebec (*top left*)

Salamanca cabriolet
takes the Prince to a
Scout Rally (*bottom
left*)

Victory drive, Kew,
1919, the Prince
of Wales at the wheel
(*opp. right*)

Silver Ghost as a tender for Rolls-Royce 'R' engine used in successful world-record flight by Flight-Lieut. Stainforth (left), 1931 (*top left*)

R talks to the men flying the 'R' engine (*top right*)

H.M.S. Chesapeake, one of the twelve Ghost armoured cars in the Libyan campaign, 1915–16 (*bottom left*)

H.M. King George V, in France during
World War I (*left*)

Ghost ambulance, chassis no. 1766,
originally with a landaulet body (*right*)

Mr Stanley Sears' 1912 Hooper limousine, chassis no. 1721 (*top left*)

1911 limousine, chassis no. 1543, owned by Mr W. F. Watson, M.A. (*top right*)

1914, London–Edinburgh type, chassis no. 27BD, now owned by Mr Clarence Kay, California (*bottom right*)

D. W. and M. R. Neale's 1910 Fuller limousine (*left*)

1912 Barker limousine, ex-Sword collection, now owned by Mr de Ferranti

Ghost crankshaft milling operations,
Derby Works, 1908

No. 1 Shop, Derby Works, group of
small capstan lathes

The men who made Ghosts. No. 1 Gate, Derby, 1910

Conduit-Street Showrooms celebrate first Transatlantic flight in Alcock and Brown's Vickers
Vimy using Rolls-Royce 'Eagle' engines

INSTRUCTIONS

FOR THE CARE OF

Rolls-Royce Cars

40-50 H.P. SIX CYLINDERS.

1907-8-9 Types.

Liable to Alteration without Notice.

—— MARCH, 1909. ——

PRICE 21|=

PUBLISHED BY

ROLLS-ROYCE, LIMITED,

DERBY, AND

14 & 15, CONDUIT STREET, LONDON.

CHAPTER I.

OPERATIONS TO BE CARRIED OUT

EVERY 250 MILES,

or if the car has run less than 250 miles

WEEKLY.

NOTES ON LUBRICATION.

It is not always necessary to fill the larger oil cups every time, if an oil cup is still par=tially full, it will be sufficient to screw it up a few more turns until the oil is seen to exude from the bearing.

It is convenient to use an oil=can for engine oil, keeping it under the bonnet, and to use the syringe for gear oil.

Always wipe off surplus oil after lubricating.

Oil liberally without being wasteful.

NOTE.—The figures in the right hand margin of this chapter indicate the approxi=mate times necessary for the performance of each operation, the total (excluding operation 1) amounting to 1h. 56m.

Obtain syringe, oil=can, wiper, and supplies of engine oil and gear oil ... 2 min.

1. Let oil from oil tank into well of crank=chamber up to correct level (Figs. 1 and 2, pp. 18 and 19) ...   ...   —

2. Re=fill oil tank with engine oil (Fig. 3, p. 19)   ...   . 3 min.

3. Add a syringe=full of gear oil to the gear box (p. 20), replace plug and screw tight   ...   . 2 min.

4. Add gear oil to the bevel gear case on back axle (preferably when the box is warm after running) (Fig. 4, p. 20), replace plug and screw tight ... 2 min.

5. Inject gear oil into the four hub caps with syringe (Figs. 5 & 6, p. 21) until the oil runs out at the screw hole (too much may cause leakage on to the tyres), replace the screws and screw tight ... ... 3 min.

6. Inject a syringe=full of gear oil into the two universal joints respec= tively at front end and at back end of propeller shaft (Figs. 6a, 6b, 7 and 8, pp. 22 and 23), replace plugs and screw tight ... ... 6 min.

7. Inject a syringe=full of gear oil into the clutch=coupling sleeve between engine and gear box (Fig. 9, p. 24) ... ·1 min.

Fill with GEAR oil the following cups, screwing each one down till you feel a resistance or see oil exuding from the bearing :—

8. Cup on front end of torque rods (Fig. 10, p. 24) ... ...
9. Two cups at back ends of torque rods (Figs. 11 and 12, p. 25) } 4 min.

10. Two cups (one at each end) of the radius rod on one side (Figs. 13 and 14, p. 26) ... ... 4 min.

11. Do the same on the other side of the car ... ... 4 min.

12. Two cups of the bearings (one each side) which support the back axle on the springs (Figs. 15 and 15a, p. 27) ... ... 2 min.

13. Fill with gear oil FOURTEEN small cups on the ends of the road springs and their shackles (Figs. 16=19 inclusive, pp. 28 and 29); these cups should then be screwed right home so as not to be shaken off ... ... 19 min.

6

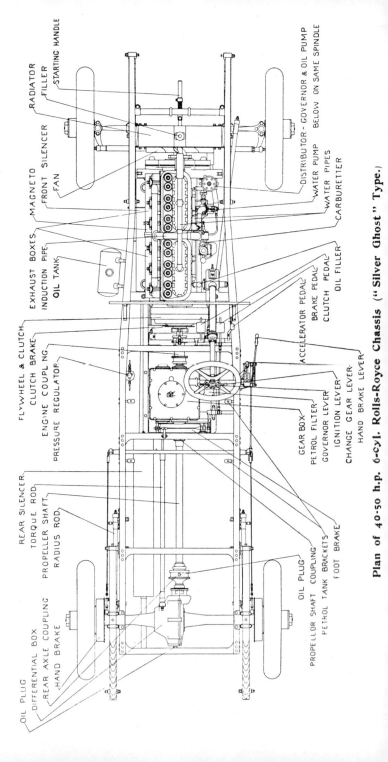

Plan of 40·50 h.p. Rolls-Royce Chassis ("Silver Ghost" Type.)

14. Fill cup over starting handle with gear oil (Fig. 20, p. 30), and screw it down till the oil is seen exuding at the other end of the shaft where it rests on the crank=shaft ... ... 2 min.

15. Fill with gear oil the cups on the TWO steering pivots (Fig. 21, p. 30) 2 min.

15a. In earlier cars not fitted with large oil cups over the steering pivots, gear oil should also be applied by syringe to the bottom surfaces as shown in Fig. 22, (p. 31) ... ... 1 min.

16. Fill with gear oil the TWO cups—one at each end—of the cross steering tube (see B in Fig. 22, p. 31), and screw down till you feel a resistance or see oil exuding from the bearings ... ... 3 min.

17. Do the same with the TWO cups—one at each end—of the longitudinal steering rod (see A Fig. 22, p. 31) ... ... 3 min.

18. Do the same with the cup on the bottom bearing of steering column, if there is one (not fitted to all types) 2 min.

19. Take off cover on front of steering box, and inject a syringe=full of gear oil, directing it carefully on to the working parts (Fig. 23, p. 32); replace cover ... ... 3 min.

20. Fill with gear oil the small cup on the steering column (ball=thrust bearing) (Fig. 24, p. 32) ... 1 min.

21. Apply a few drops of gear oil to the control mechanism on steering wheel, at points shown in Fig. 25 (p. 33) ... ... 2 min.

7

22. Fill with gear oil the cup on fan-bearing, behind radiator (Fig. 26, p. 33) ... ... 1 min.

23. Insert a teaspoonful of engine oil into the oil cup on side of commutator (Fig. 27, p. 34) ... ... 1 min.

24. Inject half a syringe=full of engine oil into the plug=hole on the governor case (see A Fig. 28, p. 34), replacing screw plug ... ... 2 min.

25. Do the same with the plug-hole (two in earlier types), and aluminium case enclosing timing gear at front of engine (Figs. 29 and 30, p. 35); replace screw plug ... ... 2 min.

26. Fill with gear oil the TWO small cups on the water pump (see C Fig. 31, p. 36), afterwards screwing them right down to make water-tight joints ... ... 5 min.

27. Drop a very few drops of engine oil (fortnightly sufficient) into the four cups on the magneto, first lifting up the lids (Figs. 32 and 33, pp. 36 and 37) ... ... 2 min.

28. Fill with gear oil the small cup on the friction brake of the magneto drive, in cars where this type is fitted (see C Fig. 34, p. 37)... ... ... 1 min.

or

28a. In later types, where the "flywheel" form of magneto = brake is fitted, apply a few drops of gear oil at the point as indicated in Fig. 35 (p. 38) 1 min.

29. Insert with syringe half a teaspoonful of gear oil into each of the TWO universal joints of the magneto shaft (A and B Fig. 36, p. 37) ... 1 min.

8

30. Do the same to each of the universal joints of the pump shaft (Fig. 37, p. 39, and B Fig. 28, p. 34)... 1 min.

31. Apply a few drops of engine oil to the SIX links and pins connecting the throttle with governor ; these are marked E in Fig. 38 (p. 40) ... ... 1 min.

32. Do the same to the throttle stem (D Fig. 39 p. 40) of the carburettor.

33. Do the same to the TWO con=necting links (F Fig. 40, p. 41) of the ignition advancing gear ... ... } 1 min.

Apply with syringe a few drops of GEAR oil to each of the following points :—

34. ELEVEN connecting points of the control mechanism at side of engine marked A, B, C, D, E, F, H, I, J, J, in Fig. 41 (p. 41) ... 2 min.

35. SIX points of the clutch mechanism which are shown in Figs. 42 to 47 inclusive (pp. 42 to 44)... ... ... 1 min.

36. Pedal mechanism at the FOUR points shown in Figs. 48 to 51 inclusive (pp. 45 and 46)... 2 min.

37. The FIVE links of the foot brake mechanism (points C in Fig. 52, p. 47) ... ... 2 min.

38. The bearing of the side brake lever (Fig. 53, p. 47). See first that the hole is free of dirt.

39. The pawl of the side brake lever (Fig. 54, p. 48).

40. The TWO connecting pins of the side brake, on "off" side of car, shown in Figs. 55 and 56 (pp. 48, 49). } 1 min.

9

41. The connecting pin B of side brakes AND the brake con=nection C (Fig. 57, p 49).

42. Do the same on the other side of the car. } 1 min.

43. Fill with gear oil the cup on the bearing of the change gear lever (Fig. 58, p. 50) ... ... 1 min.

44. Jack up driving wheel of car, inject paraffin into side brake mechan=ism (inserting nozzle of syringe be=tween brake drum and disc or cover), then spin wheel round so as to clean it out and avoid rusting of internal pins, etc. (p. 50) ... ... 4 min.

45. Do the same on the other side of the car ... ... 4 min.

46. If detachable wheels are fitted, test these for side=play, while car is still on jack, and tighten up if at all loose (p. 50) ... ... 4 min.

47. Clean internal contact face of high=tension distributor ring of bat=tery ignition (pp. 50 to 52) ... ... 2 min.

48. Open the water drain cock under the petrol filter below floor boards (Fig. 63, p. 53) (also one under pressure=feed regulator, if fitted, but this is not usual), allow it to drain a little, then close ... ... 3 min.

TOTAL ... ...1h. 56m.

NOTE.—The filling of the engine well from the oil tank is not included, as this can be done conjointly with other operations and if necessary while the car is running (though in the latter case the overflow cock must not remain open).

N.B.—The above 48 operations are fully dealt with and illustrrted in APPENDIX I. (pp. 18 to 53).

9

10

CHAPTER II.

OPERATIONS TO BE CARRIED OUT

EVERY 1,000 MILES

or if the car has run less than 1,000 miles in that time

MONTHLY.

NOTE. — The figures in the right hand margin of this chapter indicate the approximate times necessary for the performance of each operation, the total amounting to—

    (If wood wheels) ... ... 3h. 30m.
    (If wire wheels) ... ... 4h. 10m.

The time for letting the water and oil run out (23 min.) has not been counted, as this can proceed simultaneously with other work.

The total does not include charging the accumulators.

If re-adjustment of trembler is necessary, add 15 min.

If fan belt has to be shortened (by taking piece out) add 28 min.

Obtain syringe, wiper, supplies of gear oil, engine oil, and necessary tools ... ... 4 min.

1. Charge all accumulators fully (p. 54). See that bottom of accumulator box is clean and dry ... ... 2 min.

2. Take out, examine, and clean sparking plugs, re-setting the points according to gauge (pp. 54 and 55) 30 min.

3. Empty the oil from engine, clean oil-well and oil-filter (pp. 55 and 56); fill up with fresh engine oil ... 1 hr.

4. Drain out radiator and water system thoroughly, and fill up with clean soft water (pp. 57 and 58) ... 15 min.

5. If detachable wire wheels are fitted, jack up and take off all four, thoroughly clean and lubricate with gear oil the interior of the outer hubs and the exterior of the inner hubs (clean also inside hub of spare wheel) (pp. 58 and 59) ... ... 40 min.

6. Remove cover of side brake mechanism and apply a few drops of gear oil to each of the SEVEN points marked D in Fig. 70 (p. 59) ... ... 10 min.

7. Do the same on the other side of car ... ... 10 min.

8. Feel fan belt and tighten if too loose (Fig. 71 and 72, p. 60)... ... 1 min.

9. Apply with syringe a few drops of gear oil to the pins of the brackets supporting front of engine on each side of the car (Fig. 73, p. 60) ... 1 min.

10. Lubricate the leaves of the SIX road springs ; this can be done by brushing a liberal supply of gear oil along the edges of the leaves on each side, and is best effected by jacking up the frame under each spring (Figs. 74 and 75, pp. 61 and 62) ... ... 60 min.

11. Take out (carefully) and clean supplementary air-valve; do not put any oil on it (Figs. 76 and 77, pp. 62 and 63) ... ... 3 min.

12. Clean and test setting of platinum points of low-tension contact breaker on magneto ignition, re-setting if necessary (Fig. 78, p. 64). Time, without re-setting, 10 min. ; including re-setting ... ... 20 min.

13. Do the same on the battery ignition (Figs. 79 to 86, pp. 65 to 87). Without re-setting 5 min.; including re-setting ...   . 10 min.

14. Clean contact faces of high tension distributor on magneto (Fig. 87, p. 69)   ...   . 2 min.

15. Examine trembler, but do not touch the adjustment unless absolutely sure this is necessary (Fig. 88, pp. 70 and 71)   ...   . 2 min. (15 min. if adjustment necessary, which is rare)

16. Replace accumulators when fully charged; clean their tops. Reverse the direction of current by changing over the wires leading to them, i.e., connecting them up in the opposite way to that in which they were before (p. 72)   ...   . 3 min.
TOTAL ... 4 hr. 10 min.*

N.B.—The above 16 operations are fully dealt with and illustrated in APPENDIX II. (pp. 54 to 72).

* Including wire wheels.

CHAPTER III.

OPERATIONS TO BE CARRIED OUT

EVERY 5,000 MILES, OR HALF-YEARLY.

1. Take off front wheels (also inner hubs if detachable wheels are fitted), carefully clean and examine the ball races to see that there are no traces of rust (caused by water entering) lubricate thoroughly with gear oil and replace carefully; this should only be done by a skilled fitter (see Fig. 88a, p. 73).

2. Test and note the compressions of each cylinder by holding the starting-handle up against each compression in turn (Fig. 89, p. 75).

3. Take off valve covers and inspect (with lamp) interior of each cylinder, see that there has been sufficient lubrication and not too much oil (indicated by carbon deposit) (pp. 75 and 76).

4. If the compressions are bad, grind valves if necessary (pp. 76 to 78).

5. Check the adjustment of tappets after replacing valves (pp. 78 and 79).

6. Take top off (3 screws) the pressure-feed regulator (p. 79), under floor board on left-hand side of car, take out and clean with paraffin the two small valves and see that the gauze is clean.

7. Test adjustment of foot-brake (pp. 81 and 82), see that brake pedal does not touch the floor when applied hard.

8. Test adjustment of side brakes (pp. 82 to 84), see that hand lever does not come up against the end when applied hard.

9. Examine and test (for looseness) the steering gear, torque rods, and spring clips (pp. 84 and 85).

10. Take out and clean the main petrol filter under floor board, be careful to make tight joint after (p. 85).

11. Clean bottom of petrol tank (inside).

12. Clean petrol filter in top of petrol tank, refit carefully (p. 86).

13. Clean out float chamber of carburettor and float-feed valve (Figs. 110 and 111, p. 88).

14. Get underneath and examine the whole car for loose nuts, etc.

N.B.—The above 10 operations are fully dealt with and illustrated in the APPENDIX III. (pp. 73 to 88).

CHAPTER IV.

EVERY 20,000 MILES, OR TWO YEARS.

It is recommended as the safest and most economical course to send a car to its makers for dismantlement and report at least once every 20,000 miles.

N.B.—This matter is further dealt with in APPENDIX IV. (p. 89).

CHAPTER V.

INSTRUCTIONS FOR STARTING, STOPPING, etc.

STARTING.

Fill with petrol, oil and water (use the right sort of oil) (pp. 89, 90, 91, 92 and 93).

See that gear lever is in neutral position (Fig. 118, p. 94).

Give hand pump on dashboard a few strokes (Fig. 120, p. 95) sufficient to show some pressure on the gauge.

Turn on petrol tap (vertical position) (Fig. 119, p. 94).

"Flood" carburettor by depressing top of float (Fig. 121, p. 95).

Inject spoonful of petrol through tap in inlet pipe (Fig. 123, p. 96) (only if starting is difficult); shut tap again (vertical).

Place "ignition" lever in "late" position (right at the bottom), "governor" lever about a third-way up the quadrant, and carburettor lever (on dashboard) towards "strong" position (Fig. 120, p. 95).

Switch both ignitions "on."

Give starting handle a few sharp upward pulls (Fig. 122, p. 96).

When engine has started, switch off battery ignition (except for slow running), place ignition lever about half-way up, and bring governor lever back towards the "slow" position until engine runs at a slow speed; accelerate when required with the small foot pedal (Fig. 124, p. 97).

See that pressure gauge on right-hand side of dashboard shows that the oil is circulating (p. 97).

Start the car on first speed, let the clutch in gently, change on to second or third speeds as required (pp. 98 and 99), but avoid "grating" the gears.

As soon as the engine is warm move carburettor lever (on dashboard) back to the middle or towards "weak" position (see p. 97).

The ignition lever should be pushed up towards the "early" position when the engine is running fast, and brought back near the "late" position when the speed of the engine is much reduced, as when running slowly on a high gear (p. 99).

BRAKES.

To slow down when descending a hill, shut the throttle, *i.e.*, place governor lever in "slow" position (at bottom) ; the engine can then be used as a brake, the clutch being left engaged. If more brake power is required, use the hand brake in preference to the foot brake ; on long hills the hand and foot=brakes should both be used (p. 99).

STOPPING.

Before leaving the car, the gear lever should be in the "neutral" position (Fig. 125, p. 104).

The hand=brake firmly "on" (Fig. 125, p. 104).

Both switches "off," and the petrol tap "off."

All lamps (if alight) extinguished.

GENERAL.

Charge the accumulators at least monthly (whether used or not).

Inject a little oil on to surface of clutch when it shows signs of "fierceness," but do not run with a "slipping" clutch (Fig. 138, p. 118).

Do not run with the oil pressure gauge below 3 lbs.

If a chattering noise (in older types) is heard at the magneto, tighten the nut on the magneto "brake" slightly, and well lubricate the magneto brake (p. 105). (See also remarks concerning "Flywheel and Brake of Magneto," pp. 105 and 106.)

N.B.—The contents of this chapter are fully dealt with and illustrated in APPENDIX V. (pp. 89 to 107).

APPENDIX I.

NOTE.—The foregoing simple instructions, if intelligently followed, are all that are necessary for working the ROLLS-ROYCE cars ; the following Appendix is given for the benefit of anyone wishing to make a closer study of the mechanism.

Concerning the Operations Enumerated in Chapter I.

EVERY 250 MILES OR WEEKLY.

The Numbers of the Operations correspond with those in Chapter I.

1. **Replenishing Crank Chamber.**

The correct level of oil in the well is important, and is indicated by a special overflow cock (D Fig. 65, p. 56) fixed on the lower half of the crank-chamber, in rear of the oil well ; this cock is operated by a small lever which will be found fixed to the chassis frame below a brass tank on the left side

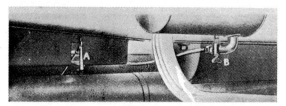

FIG. 1.
OVERFLOW COCK A CLOSED.

of the car (Fig. 1) ; it is closed when the lever is vertical (A in Fig. 1). This overflow cock indicates the normal height of the oil when the car is *level* ; the oil when the engine is still should not be filled in above this level, otherwise it would be disastrous when mounting hills, and it should not be allowed to get *much below* this level or the pump would fail to properly keep up the circulation.

It is wise to open the overflow cock *daily* to see if oil runs out (do not be deceived by a small amount of oil which may be in the cock itself); if none flows out (and you are satisfied that the cock-hole is not clogged by dirt), the level is getting low and more oil is required in the engine-well.

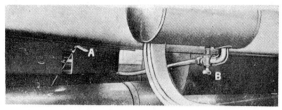

FIG. 2.

OVERFLOW COCK A OPEN.

Before turning on the oil supply to the engine, this overflow cock should be open as shown at A in Fig. 2 ; to let oil into the engine-well the tap B of the oil tank in Fig. 2 should then be turned on and left on (the oil runs into the engine *very slowly*, and may take several hours)

2. Refilling Supplementary Oil Tank.

FIG. 3.

FILLING OIL TANK WITH ENGINE OIL.

until the oil begins to run out at the overflow cock (the car should be level or this will not be a true indication ; both the overflow cock and the oil supply tap should then be turned off, the latter is off when at right angles to the pipe. (For further information see pp. 55 and 110).

3. Change Gear-box.

The change gear-box should contain about six pints of heavy gear oil. The oil should just cover the reverse spindle which can be seen by taking off the inspection cover. Do not allow the level of oil in the gear-box to get low. The correct level of the oil is 6 inches below the surface of the inspection hole ; when making this measurement take care that time has been given for the oil to settle and the froth to disappear ; the measurement can be made through the small plug hole in the top of the gear box without removing the inspection cover. "A little oil and often" is the best practice—say $\frac{1}{4}$ to $\frac{1}{2}$ pint every 250 miles or weekly. Replace plug and screw tight.

4. Bevel Gear-box.

The back-axle gear-box should contain about $4\frac{1}{2}$ pints of heavy gear. oil. The oil should be filled in at the back filling plug (Fig. 4) until it runs out at this plug. When

FIG. 4.

FILLING BEVEL GEAR-CASE WITH GEAR OIL.

opening the filling hole, do not be deceived by a little congealed oil, or by froth, both of which may give the appearance of the box being full. Fill same quantities and at same times as the change gear-box, *i.e.*, $\frac{1}{4}$ to $\frac{1}{2}$ a pint injected with a syringe every 250 miles or once a week.

Before filling the bevel gear-box it is convenient, especially in cold weather, to warm the oil to make it flow easily. It is also best to fill the box when it is warm, *i.e.*, when the car has just come in.

If it is desired to fill the box when cold, and the oil is very thick, it is advisable to jack up one wheel and turn it round, so that the bevel gear by revolving will help to disperse the oil inside.

If too high a level of oil is allowed in either of the gearboxes, waste and trouble will follow, as the violent agitation causes froth to form, and the bulk of the oil is so increased as to ooze out of the bearings and to get on to the brakes and tyres.

N.B.—Do not on any account use grease in the gearboxes, as this would clog the oil passages.

5. Hub Caps.

Inject oil until it begins to overflow at the screw hole. If the hub caps are taken off, they should be screwed up

FIG. 5.
INJECT GEAR OIL UP TO SCREW HOLE.

FIG. 6.
INJECT GEAR OIL UP TO SCREW HOLE.

so as to make an oil-tight joint. (Note that the "off" side caps on ordinary wood wheels have left-hand thread.) If grease be used it may block up the overflow ducts, and cause oil to get on to the side brakes and tyres. For wire wheels see special notes on pp. 58 and 152.

FIG. 6a.
SHOWING OIL PLUG IN COVER AT FORE END OF PROPELLER SHAFT.

FIG. 6b.
FORWARD END UNIVERSAL JOINT OF PROPELLOR SHAFT.

6. Propeller Shaft.

The universal joints of the propeller shaft, which are at *each* end, are covered in, and a brass oil plug is screwed into the cover. See that the covers at each end and the filling plugs make oil-tight joints.

These universal joints have case-hardened wearing surfaces, and if really well lubricated they will wear a very long time without becoming slack ; whereas if they are neglected they will wear more in an hour than they

FIG. 7.

INJECT SYRINGE-FULL OF GEAR OIL AT B (FRONT END OF PROPELLER SHAFT).

FIG. 8.

INJECT SYRINGE-FULL OF GEAR OIL AT A (REAR END OF PROPELLER SHAFT).

should otherwise in a year. It is astonishing how often we have found these parts entirely neglected. The joints close behind the gear-box require more than the others. Care must be taken, however, not to let any oil get on to the foot-brake.

7. **Clutch Coupling.**

The oil hole is in the centre of the coupling body.

FIG. 9.

INJECT SYRINGE-FULL OF GEAR OIL INTO CLUTCH COUPLING.

Should oil at any time be found to leak out round the castellated nuts, these should be tightened.

8. **Torque Rod (front end).**

FIG. 10.

A SHOWS CUP ON FRONT END OF TORQUE RODS (GEAR OIL).

9. Torque Rod (rear end).

FIG. 11.

UPPER OIL CUP (FOR GEAR OIL) AT REAR END OF TORQUE ROD.

THERE IS ANOTHER SIMILAR CUP AT BOTTOM.

FIG. 12.

C AND D (FIG. 12) SHOW CUPS ON BOTH REAR ENDS OF TORQUE RODS (GEAR OIL).

10. Radius Rods (near side).

FIG. 13.

CUP ON FRONT END OF NEAR SIDE RADIUS ROD (GEAR OIL)

FIG. 14.

CAP AT REAR END OF RADIUS ROD (GEAR OIL).

11. **Radius Rods (off side).**

Same cups on radius rod, other side of car.

12. **Back Axle and Spring Bracket Joint.**

FIG. 15.

A AND B (FIG. 15) SHOW OIL CUPS OF BRACKETS WHICH
SUPPORT BACK AXLE ON SPRINGS.

FIG. 15a.

SCREWING UP GREASE ON BACK AXLE.

13. **Spring Shackles.**

The fourteen small cups are shown in the following Figs.
16-19 (inclusive); after filling with *gear* oil, they should be
screwed right up so that all the oil is squeezed out, to
prevent their unscrewing through vibration.

FIG. 16.

TWO CUPS ON FRONT OF "OFF" HIND SPRING (SAME ON
OTHER SIDE).

FIG. 17.

TWO CUPS ON BACK OF "NEAR" HIND SPRING
(SAME ON OTHER SIDE).

FIG. 18.

CUPS ON FRONT OF "NEAR" FRONT SPRING
(SAME ON OTHER SIDE).

FIG. 19.

TWO CUPS ON BACK OF "OFF" FRONT SPRING
(SAME ON OTHER SIDE).

14. **Starting Handle.**

The cup on starting handle should be screwed down till the gear oil is squeezed out at the other end where it rests on the spigot of the crank shaft.

FIG. 20.
OIL CUP ON STARTING HANDLE.

15. **Steering Pivots.**

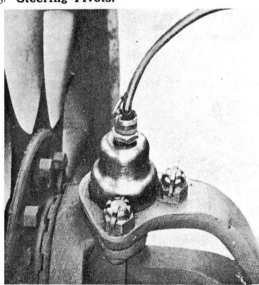

FIG. 21.
FILLING WITH GEAR OIL ONE OF THE TWO FRONT
AXLE PIVOTS.

15A.

In cars not fitted with large oil cups over the steering pivots, gear oil should also be applied by syringe to the bottom surfaces as shown in Fig. 22.

16.

Cross Steering Tube, cup for gear oil at *each* end. B in Fig. 22 shows the one on "off" side.

FIG. 22.

OILING BOTTOM OF STEERING PIVOTS.

17.

Longitudinal Steering Tube, cup for gear oil at *each* end. A in Fig. 22 shows the one on forward end.

18.

Bottom bearing of **steering column,** cup (on some types only) to be filled with gear oil.

19. **Steering Box.**

FIG. 23.

STEERING BOX WITH COVER REMOVED, SHOWING METHOD OF INJECTING GEAR OIL ON TO WORKING PARTS.

20. **Steering Column.**

FIG. 24.

CUP FOR GEAR OIL ON BALL-THRUST BEARING OF STEERING COLUMN.

21. Control on Steering Wheel.

FIG. 25.

THE ARROWS IN FIG. 25 SHOW WHERE GEAR OIL SHOULD BE APPLIED TO THE CONTROL MECHANISM ON STEERING WHEEL.

22. Fan Bearing.

FIG. 26.

CUP D (FIG. 26) FOR GEAR OIL ON FAN BEARING.

23. Commutator.

FIG. 27.

CUP FOR ENGINE OIL, WITH FLAP, ON SIDE OF COMMUTATOR.

24. Governor.

FIG. 28.

A SHOWS PLUG-HOLE FOR GOVERNOR CASE ($\frac{1}{2}$-SYRINGE OF GEAR OIL).

25. Timing Gear.

This in the earlier types is lubricated by injecting half a syringe full of gear oil into each of the two plug-holes shown in Figs. 29 and 30; in later types there is only one plug-hole.

FIG. 29.
OILING TIMING GEAR.

FIG. 30.
OILING TIMING GEAR.

26. Water Pump.

The two cups, C, C, in Fig. 31, when filled with gear oil, should be screwed *right* down, and there should be a leather disc in the bottom of each cup so as to make a water-tight joint.

FIG. 31.
C, C, WATER PUMP LUBRICATORS.

27. Magneto.

FIG. 32.
MAGNETO LUBRICATORS A AND B.

The magneto should be studied in order that the various small points where lubrication is required are not overlooked ; they are somewhat difficult to get at, but are none the less important. The magneto is fitted with ball bearings throughout.

FIG. 33.
MAGNETO LUBRICATORS A, B AND C.

These ball bearings must be lubricated at least twice each month by injecting a few drops of *engine* oil at the places marked "oil." There are four oil lids, these are shown at A and B in Fig. 32, and A, B and C in Fig. 33.

28A. Magneto Brake.

The oil cup for earlier form is shown at C in Fig. 34 (gear oil).

FIG. 34.
OILER C FOR OLD TYPE MAGNETO BRAKE.
or

28B.

In the new type "fly-wheel" form of magneto brake, a few drops of gear oil should be applied at the point indicated by the line in Fig. 35.

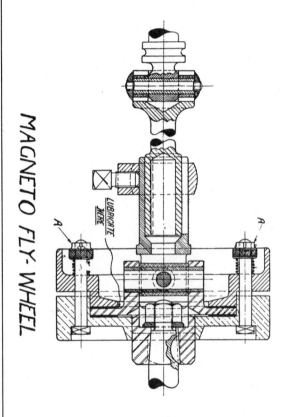

Fig. 35.
LUBRICATION OF NEW TYPE MAGNETO BRAKE.

29. Magneto Drive.

Each of the universal joints A and B, Fig. 36 to have gear oil ($\frac{1}{2}$-teaspoonful).

FIG. 36.
UNIVERSAL JOINTS A AND B OF MAGNETO DRIVE.

NOTE.—Some of the lubrication points of the magneto and its " drive " enumerated above, are often overlooked.

All the rest of the parts of the magneto itself require no lubrication ; and it may be pointed out that the contact breaker is designed to work without oil.

30.

FIG. 37.
OILING UNIVERSAL JOINT OF PUMP DRIVE (GEAR OIL).
(Also see B, Fig. 28.)

31. Control Mechanism.

NOTE :—The driver, on first taking over a new Rolls-Royce car, would do well to trace out the various movements and connections between the governor lever on the steering wheel, the accelerator pedal, the automatic governor, and the throttle valve on the carburettor ;

FIG. 38.
SIX POINTS E CONNECTING THROTTLE WITH GOVERNOR
TO BE OILED WITH GEAR OIL.

32.

FIG. 39.
THROTTLE STEM D TO BE LUBRICATED WITH ENGINE OIL.

all these are directly or indirectly connected together, and care should be taken to oil, every week, the numerous connecting links, pivots and pins carefully ; the perfect governing of the engine, after the car has been in use for a long time will much depend upon careful attention to such details, which will avoid unnecessary wear and "play" in these parts. The same applies to the moving parts between the ignition lever on the steering wheel and the commutator.

N.B.—These links should be quite free and should "float."

33. Ignition Advance Gear.

FIG. 40.

ENGINE OIL TO BE APPLIED TO THE TWO POINTS, F, F, OF THE IGNITION—ADVANCE GEAR. (SEE NOTE UNDER § 31, p. 40.)

34. Control Mechanism.

FIG. 41.

11 CONNECTING POINTS OF THE CONTROL MECHANISM A, B, C, D, E, F, H, I, J, J, J, (GEAR OIL).

35. Clutch Mechanism.

The six points shown in the following Figs. 42 to 47 (inclusive) to have gear oil.

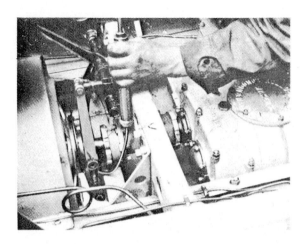

FIG. 42.

LUBRICATING CLUTCH MECHANISM.

FIG. 43.

LUBRICATING CLUTCH MECHANISM.

36. **Pedal Mechanism.**

The four points shown in following Figs. 48 to 51 (inclusive) to have gear oil.

FIG. 48.

LUBRICATING PEDAL MECHANISM.

FIG. 49.

LUBRICATING PEDAL MECHANISM.

FIG. 50.

LUBRICATING PEDAL MECHANISM

FIG. 51.

LUBRICATING PEDAL MECHANISM.

37. **Foot-Brake Mechanism.**

FIG. 52.
LUBRICATE 5 LINKS, C, WITH GEAR OIL,

38. **Side Brake Lever.**
See first that the hole is free of dirt.

FIG. 53.
LUBRICATING BRAKE LEVER BEARING.

39. **Pawl of Brake Lever.**

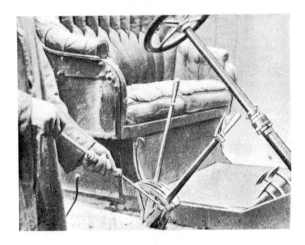

FIG. 54.
LUBRICATING CATCH OF BRAKE LEVER.

40. **Side Brake Connecting Rod.**

FIG. 55.
OILING FRONT END (GEAR OIL).

FIG. 56.
OILING REAR END (GEAR OIL).

41. Side Brake Connections.

FIG. 57.
APPLY GEAR OIL TO CONNECTIONS B & C (OFF SIDE).

42. Side Brake Connections on Near Side of Car.

43. Gear Lever.

FIG. 58.
FILLING CUP ON BEARING (GEAR OIL).

44. Side Brakes.

Jack up driving wheel of car, inject paraffin into side bra e mechanism (inserting nozzle of syringe between brake drum and disc or cover) ; then spin wheel round so as to clean it out, and avoid rusting of internal pins, etc.

45. Do the same on the other side of the car.

46. Detachable Wheels.

If these are fitted, they should be examined frequently and felt to see if there is any side-shake ; any play should at once be taken up, for if they are allowed to run when loose un lue wear will result. (See p. 58).

47. Cleaning Distributor of Battery Ignition.

The internal face of the distributor ring, on which the carbon brush rubs, should be cleaned with a dry rag.

The following illustrations show how to get at the distributor of the battery ignition :

FIG. 59.

PULL OUT HIGH-TENSION TERMINALS.

FIG. 60.

HAVING PUSHED WIRES TO ONE SIDE, PULL OFF THE 2 CLIPS.

FIG. 61.

REMOVE THE HIGH-TENSION COVER.

FIG. 62.

Lift off distributor ring, the internal face of which can then be easily cleaned, for which a dry rag should be used. Carbon dust or moisture on the distributor will cause pre-ignition.

NOTE.—It is sometimes found that the tendency to pre-ignite from this cause is reduced by very *slightly* smearing the surfaces with engine oil after cleaning them.

48. **Water Drain.**

This drain tap, below main filter, is opened by unscrewing ; a little petrol should be allowed to flow out before closing. In some early types the drain cock under the pressure feed regulator should also be opened for clearing purposes, and closed.

Fig. 63.

WATER DRAIN, A, UNDER PETROL FILTER.

Note on Lubrication.

It is not always necessary to actually *re-fill* the larger oil cups every 250 miles or weekly ; if an oil cup is still partially full, it will be sufficient to screw it up a few more turns until the gear oil is seen to exude from the bearing.

The smaller grease cups on these cars are intended to be filled up and screwed home tight, so as to avoid the cap falling off and avoid the unsatisfactory locking devices usually supplied with these little lubricators.

Pay special attention to details. We often find on examining a car that although the main bearings have been well cared for, some inconspicuous points, where but slight movement takes place, have been entirely neglected.

It is convenient to use the oil-can for engine oil, and the syringe for gear oil, keeping both under the bonnet (for warmth).

Wipe off surplus oil after lubricating.

Oil *liberally* without being wasteful.

APPENDIX II.

Concerning the operations enumerated in Chapter II.

EVERY 1,000 MILES OR MONTHLY.

The Numbers of the Operations correspond with those in Chapter II.

1. **Accumulators.**

Do not wait till the accumulators "give out" ; test them occasionally with a voltmeter ; each element should record not less than two volts. A cell will work as low as 1·8 per element, but they should not be allowed to run lower than 1·9 volts each element. A test to be a fair one should be made immediately after the engine has been running at least a minute.

Before unscrewing the terminals, note how the wires are connected up ; the batteries should be charged with "continuous" current at a rate *not higher* than the maximum mentioned in the instructions on the accumulator case, the small bungs or plugs should be removed while charging. Clean the bottom of the battery box on car.

Batteries should be charged about once a month *whether used or not.*

When batteries are quite new they should be charged very frequently at first, say once a week.

See special instructions in Appendix on "Care of Accumulators."—P. 158, *et seq.*

2. **Sparking Plugs.**

To take out a sparking plug slip off the wire and screw plug out with special key provided.

Examine each plug ; see to the following :—

(1) The points should not be coated with oil (clean them in petrol).

(2) The insulation should not be wet, cracked or coated with carbon.

(3) There should not be any beads formed by melted metal on the centre stem, or any sharp corners or "burrs" on inside end of the plug ; these becoming incandescent would cause pre-ignitions.

(4) The gap at the points should be correct ; to allow for burning apart these should be set at .01 inch

for the magneto plugs, and ·02 inch for the battery plugs. A special gauge is now provided for these measurements. All gaps of the plugs of the same ignition should be equal.

(5) Special sparking plugs should be used for the magneto ignition, which are different to those used for the battery ignition. Plugs of the "Pognon" make intended for the magneto ignition are marked "M."

NOTE.—Magneto plugs may be used for the battery ignition but not *vice versa*.

(6) It should be noted that the battery plugs should be situated over the inlet valves, and the magneto plugs over the exhaust valves; we have sometimes noticed clients' cars on which these have been changed over in error.

FIG. 64.
SLIPPING WIRE OFF SPARKING PLUG.

3. Oil-Well and Filter.

Unscrew with spanner the drain plug fixed in the centre of the cover of the oil-well A (Fig. 65) and let all oil out of the engine well or "sump;" then take down and clean the cover A, the filter B and suction pipe C.

Then replace filter in the well and refix the well, taking care to make a good joint (with good stout paper) on to the crank-chamber; see also that the unions of the oil pipes are screwed up tight, then refill the well with a *fresh* charge of engine oil from the side tank up to the overflow level; if preferred, the port G in Fig. 66 may be used for refilling, to save time.

Whenever the oil-well, pipes, or pump are taken down for any purpose and put back again, special care should be taken when first starting the engine up (after refilling)

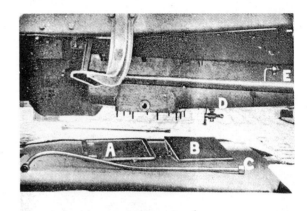

FIG. 65.
TAKING DOWN OIL-WELL AND FILTER.

FIG. 66.
G SHOWS FILTER FOR CRANK-CHAMBER.

to see that the pressure gauge reads correctly, for an "air lock" may form which will prevent the flow of oil. Should this occur the pipes should be "primed," by unscrewing one of the unions leading from the trunk pipe to the crankshaft, or the special plug (Fig. 67) provided in some types, and injecting oil therein by means of the oil-syringe, or it may

Fig. 67.
"Priming" the Oil Pipes after Refilling.

be poured in from an oil-can (with patience). The unions can then be refixed and the engine started up again, but it is possible that a second attempt will be required.

4. The Water System.

Fig. 68.
E is Drain Tap for Water System.

After the water has ceased to flow (the car being level), close this tap, *i.e.*, vertical position.

Re-fill with clean *soft* water (such as pure rain-water) ; see that no straw or leaves, etc., are poured in.

Level.

The radiator should not be filled higher than two inches above the tops of the tubes, neither should the level be allowed to get much below this. The white line in Fig. 69

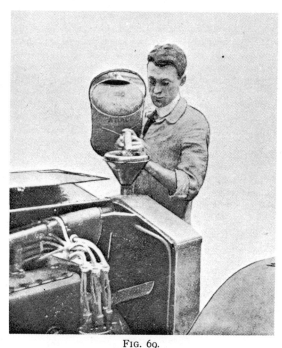

Fig. 69.
White Line shows Correct Water Level.

shows the correct level. If there is less than $3\frac{1}{2}$ inches between the top of the water and the top of the filler, the water will sometimes spray out through the cap as though it were boiling.

5. Wire Wheels.

Where detachable wire wheels are used, care should be taken to see that these are well tightened up when put on, also that the locking device is effective.

All four wheels (also the spare wheel) should be taken off

for their periodical cleaning ; the interior of the outer hubs and the exterior of the inner hubs should be carefully cleaned, then well lubricated with gear oil.

The following are the recommendations made by Messrs. Rudge-Whitworth, Ltd., concerning their detachable wheels :—

1.—After changing make sure that the wheel is home on the inner hub by looking through one of the three inspection holes in the hub of the detachable wheel.

2.—Make sure that the pawl works freely and is fully in engagement with one of the notches.

3.—See that all wheels are always kept constantly tight. To do this try periodically rocking the wheel, also try with the spanner. These precautions are necessary because sometimes dirt or grit gets in between the surfaces of wheel and inner hub when they are fitted. This grit grinds away and leaves the wheel loose. If the wheel is run loose the driving dogs and even the thread will be gradually worn away, thus practically destroying both wheel and inner hub.

4.—Each wheel should be occasionally removed to make sure that the surfaces on which the detachable part slides are thoroughly clean and well oiled.

The wheel should be put back with plenty of oil so that any water working in from the outside will not cause rust and render the removal of the wheel difficult. *See Special Caution, p. 74.*

6. **Side Brakes.**

The cover is made in two halves and can be easily removed by taking off five nuts which secure it.

FIG. 70.
SEVEN POINTS D TO BE LUBRICATED WITH GEAR OIL.

7.

Same on other side of car.

8. **Fan Belt.**

If this feels too slack, it can be tightened by loosening the clamp (Fig. 71), and turning the bracket (Fig. 72), which is mounted eccentrically, *then relocking.* Should the lever (Fig. 72) reach the end of the slot, the belt should be shortened about one inch.

FIG. 71.
UNLOCKING CLAMP OF FAN BELT BRACKET.

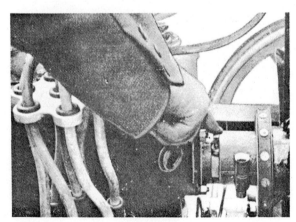

FIG. 72.
TIGHTENING FAN BELT.

9. Engine Supports.

Lubricate with gear oil.

FIG. 73.
POINTS TO BE OILED, A AND B, ON "OFF" SIDE
(SAME ON "NEAR" SIDE).

10. Road Springs.

The best method of lubricating the faces of the spring-leaves (to prevent them squeaking) is to take off the spring

FIG. 71.
TAKING OFF SPRING CLIP.

clip, then jack up the chassis *frame* (above the spring), this will cause the leaves of the spring to open slightly. Gear oil can then be smeared with a brush along the edges of the plates (on each side of the spring) and between them. Repeat the process with each of six road springs.

FIG. 75.
LUBRICATING SPRING LEAVES.

11. Air Valve.

This is got at by unscrewing two screws (Fig. 76) and taking off the cap with spring attached (Fig. 77).

FIG. 76.
UNSCREWING CAP OF AIR VALVE.

The air valve should be drawn out slowly and carefully, so as not to distort same or bend centre spindle.

It should be rubbed with a clean cloth, free from fluff ; avoid any form of lubrication.

If it is desired to test the action of the air valve, the following points may be looked to :

The diaphragm should be square and firmly attached to air valve, be flush with top of throat, *i.e.*, should open throat as soon as lifted, and should cut off throat when down.

The air valve should be sluggish without sticking (·005″ clearance) ; it should take about three seconds to close itself when pushed in close. The spring should just

FIG. 77.
TO GET AT AIR VALVE.

touch the air valve when down. It should be down at very low engine speeds, commence to rise as soon as accelerated and lift to the top at high speeds (about 1500 revs.).

There should be an air-tight joint to cover of air chamber (top side).

12. Low Tension Contact Breaker (Magneto).

The low-tension contact breaker on the magneto should be cleaned and examined carefully (Fig. 78) to see that the small lever carrying the platinum point is working *freely*, and that the platinum points are in good order and correctly

set. (The small round cap must, of course, be slipped off first.) This setting is correct when the maximum break is such that the special magneto spanner (shown in Fig. 78) will *just* go in. It is good practice to carry a spare contact breaker for the magneto.

N.B.—By pulling off the "advance" portion with the fingers, any correction of this adjustment can be made with the spanner ; the two little rollers which come off with

FIG. 78.
SHOWING LOW-TENSION CONTACT BREAKER AND SPANNER-GAUGE.

this portion should also thus be examined and felt to see if they revolve freely ; use thin clock oil for these.

A defect with the low-tension contact breaker is generally manifest by miss-fires.

13. Low-Tension Contact Breaker (Battery Ignition).

To get at this for periodical cleaning, proceed thus :—
Pull out the high-tension terminals (Fig. 79), and push

to one side, lift off the two clips which hold down the high-tension portion (Fig. 80), remove the cover (Fig. 81 and lift off the distributor ring (Fig. 82). The commutator can then be got at by pulling off the low-tension wire (Fig. 83) and removing the side cover (Fig. 84).

FIG 79.

PULLING OUT THE HIGH-TENSION WIRES.

FIG. 80.

LIFTING OFF THE TWO CLIPS.

FIG. 81.

REMOVING THE HIGH-TENSION COVER.

FIG. 82.

THE DISTRIBUTOR RING LIFTED OFF.

FIG. 83.

PULLING OFF LOW-TENSION WIRE.

The low-tension contact maker (of the battery ignition) is very rarely found to be out of order, but the following examinations can be made. Having satisfied yourself that the platinum points (Fig. 85) are clean, flat and true, and that the blade is tightened so that the platinum-pointed

FIG. 84.

REMOVING SIDE COVER.

screw is opposite the platinum on the blade, and that the blade has sufficient set upon it to push the platinum points into firm contact when the screw is correctly advanced, proceed to set the contacts in the following manner :—The high-tension distributor and side cover being removed, turn the engine round until the roller on the little actuating lever is on the lowest portion of the cam, that is to say, in the middle of one of the flat portions of the cam. Then with the platinum points screwed well apart, proceed to advance the platinum screw slowly (Fig. 86) until the trembler of the induction coil by buzzing indicates that the platinum screw has just come into contact with the platinum on the blade, then give the screw *a further half-turn* and check up the small

FIG. 85.

PLATINUM POINTS OF LOW-TENSION CONTACT BREAKER.

screw on the side which secures it. If this is correctly done the trembler will be found to work during periods amounting to a total of one-third of a revolution of the commutator, and remain stationary during a total of two-thirds, and if it fails to do so, some mistake has arisen and the platinum screw should be re-adjusted until it does so.

If, however, the trembler is kept lightly set and in good order, this low-tension contact ought not to require any attention for a whole season.

When replacing the wires on to the distributor, see that the number marked on the ebonite of each terminal corresponds with the figure marked at each hole.

FIG. 86.

ADJUSTING PLATINUM LOW-TENSION CONTACT SCREWS.

14. High=Tension Distributor (Magneto Ignition).

Fig. 87 shows the cover of the magneto distributor removed for cleaning purposes. Electrical leakage in the high-tension distributor of either the battery ignition or magneto causes pre-ignitions and can generally be cured by careful cleaning with a dry rag ; it is sometimes found that

FIG. 87.

the tendency to pre-ignite on account of carbon dust or moisture on the distributors is reduced by *very slightly* smearing the surfaces with oil after cleaning them.

NOTE.—Any defect with the distributor is generally manifest by pre-ignitions, whereas if the defect is with the low-tension contact breaker, it is manifest by mis-fires. When replacing the wires on the distributor of magneto, see that the number of rings cut in the ebonite of each terminal corresponds with the figure beside each hole.

15. Trembler of Coil.

The coil and trembler should be cleaned and *examined*, but if there is anything wrong with the running of the engine, they *should not be touched until you are sure that everything else in the ignition system is right*, as in doing so the trouble is often made worse. To get the tremblers into the best working condition is a delicate operation and, therefore, they should not be unnecessarily disturbed.

N.B.—In any case, do not pull the trembler to pieces until you have opened it with your finger and have seen that the points are really in bad contact or out of adjustment.

If one of the platinum points is deeply pitted, and the other point has assumed the shape of a cone to fit into the pit, both points should be filed with a very fine file until they are flat. In order to adjust a trembler, follow carefully the printed instructions inside the lid of the coil-box.

Re-setting Trembler.

The following is the proper method of adjusting the trembler of the induction coil (box on dashboard) :—

Having seen that the platinum points are in really first-class condition—sound, flat, clean and true—proceed to test whether the iron armature has sufficient " set " on the spring to just lift it away from the core of the coil. The amount of force should not be more than 3 or 4 grammes or $\frac{1}{10}$th oz., which is about the weight of a lead pencil of half its maximum length. This armature should also have free play of about $\frac{1}{16}$ in. between its touching the end of the core and falling back against its stop. As this part is generally arranged by the makers, unless the coil has worn to some extent or had very rough handling, it should not be necessary to make any alteration to this part.

In addition to the iron armature, there is the spring plate which carries the platinum point, to be put in place and screwed down, taking care that the two platinum points are opposite one another. This spring should have a slight upward curvature sufficient to cause the platinum points to

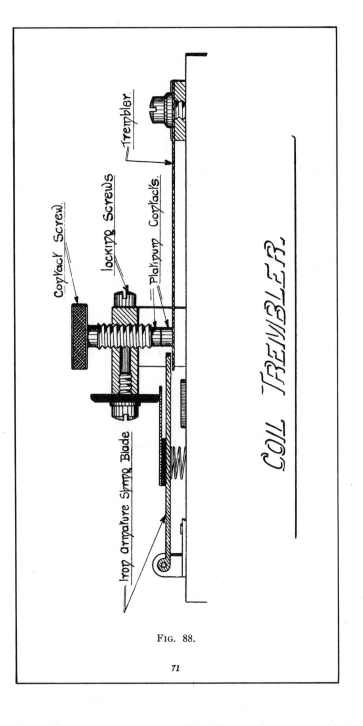

Coilyack Screw.

locking Screws

Trembler.

Platinum Coylack's.

Iron Armature Spring Blade

COIL TREMBLER.

FIG. 88.

71

make contact with a pressure of about ½ oz. or 15 grammes. Should this pressure be too great a large amount of current will be taken by the coil and the platinum points will not last well. If, however, it is too slack, it may fail to make contact sufficiently quickly when the engine is running at a fast speed.

It is the upward pressure of this spring which is the most difficult part of the adjustment to make, it being a simple matter after this is correct to follow our usual instructions as follows : —

To adjust the platinum point, start with the points quite apart, turn on the battery current, screw down the screw slowly until the action of the trembler shows that the points have just come into contact, then give the screw a further quarter of a turn which will ensure good contact and the correct amount of *play* for the iron armature viz., $\frac{1}{100}$ of an inch.

If the trembler is set with too much weight on the platinum points the coil will take an excess of current, causing not only the burning of the platinum points on the trembler but also those on the low tension commutator.

NOTE.—If the coil box is much exposed to rain and wet it should have a waterproof cover fitted.

Dirt and dust should be kept out of the coil box, and the ebonite and fittings should be carefully dusted occasionally (without upsetting the trembler adjustment).

In case of trembler troubles, the "earth" connections should be inspected to see if sound.

16. Re-installing Accumulator.

An accumulator should be left "on charge" till gas is emitted freely from *both* positive and negative plates, and each element shows 2·5 volts (immediately after the charging has been stopped, this will fall to 2·1 volts per element).

The liquid should cover the tops of the plates by at least one-eighth of an inch.

When taking over the accumulators after "charge," see that the plates are not buckled or blistered, the battery case is clean and dry, acid clear, of right density and sufficient to cover the plates. Battery terminals may be greased to prevent corrosion.

To prevent undue "pitting" of the platinum points, the direction of current should be reversed, by changing over the battery terminals, about every 1,000 miles, or each time the accumulators are being fitted after re-charging.

N.B.—See Appendix XII., p. 158, for Special Instructions on the Care of Accumulators.

APPENDIX III.

Concerning the operations enumerated in Chapter III.

EVERY 5,000 MILES OR HALF-YEARLY.

The Numbers of the operations correspond with those in Chapter III.

I. **Front Wheels.**

The ball-bearings of the *front* wheels should be taken down *at least* once every 5,000 miles (preferably more often),

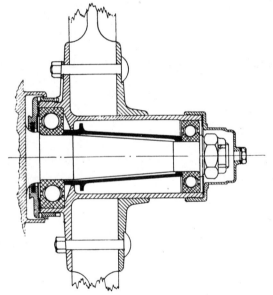

FIG. 88A.

carefully cleaned and examined for rust caused by water entering (which is extremely harmful to the ball-race).

This however should only be done at the Rolls-Royce Works, or by a thoroughly skilled fitter.

NOTE.—If there are any traces of rust, care should be taken to see that a felt washer in good condition is fitted in a

groove specially cut in the large brass cap which holds the large ball-bearing ; this is to prevent water entering.

The bearings before being replaced should be thoroughly oiled with gear oil.

CAUTION.

When replacing a wooden wheel (or in the case of wire wheels, the internal hub) on an axle it is, of course, essential to safety not to omit to replace the "distance sleeve" (shown in black in Fig. 88a), which is intended to keep separate and fix in their places the two ball bearings.

Fitting and Adjustment of Front Wheels. (Wooden).

The big ball-race should first be placed in position, so that when a "straight-edge" is placed along the top of the seating there should be $\frac{1}{64}$ in. clearance between it (the straight-edge) and the ball-race. The brass cap should then be put on (fibre washer being in position), screwed up dead tight, and locked with the plate provided for the purpose. Place the wheel on the axle and insert the distance sleeve large end first, after which the small ball-race may be put on the axle and inside the hub, this small ball-race being "distanced" from the large one by the distance sleeve previously inserted ; then put on the large plain washer and fix the whole in position by screwing up the nut tight on the thread and "split-pinning" it.

NOTES.

In the case of detachable wire wheels, the above procedure is the same for replacing the ball-bearings after dismantlement, except that the words "inner hub" should be substituted for "wheel."

It is always important to see that front wheel hubs fit their stub-axles without looseness or end play, as any excessive slackness at this point might cause a breakage through the shocks that would result.

When wooden front wheels are taken off (by coachbuilders, etc.) be careful to see that they are not changed over, and the wrong wheel put on the wrong side.

In the case of ordinary wood front wheels :—

The nut on the near side axle has a left-hand thread, and the "near" side hub cap has a right-hand thread, while the nut on the "off" side axle has a right-hand thread, and the off side hub cap has a left-hand thread.

In the case of detachable wire wheels :—

The outer hub caps (on all four wheels) are right-handed but should the *inner hubs* of the front wheels be taken off for any purpose, it should be remembered that the nut on the near-side axle has a left-hand thread, and the *inner* hub cap on the near side has a right-hand thread, while the nut on the off side axle has a right-hand thread, and the *inner* hub cap on the off side has a left-hand thread.

N.B.—For back wheels see under "Hints" p. 151.

2. Compressions.

To secure regular firing and full power, the compressions should be kept good. This can be tested by holding the starting-handle against each compression. Poor compressions are generally caused by leaky valves or valve covers. A little oil poured around the latter makes a useful test. It is best to test one cylinder at a time by

Fig. 89.
PULLING UP STARTING HANDLE SLOWLY TO TEST EACH COMPRESSION.

taking out an ignition plug from each of the five other cylinders.

In the case of the valve covers, the joints should be made with the special copper and asbestos washers ; the faces on these washers should be kept clean and flat. These covers should be screwed up with the special key provided. The thread should not be tight.

3. Cylinders.

These should be kept clean, and the periodical inspection done by taking out the valve covers and inserting a small electric lamp right into the cylinder, the valve covers being

taken off, Fig. 90. Note if there is sufficient lubrication. Caked carbon deposits in the cylinders are a sign of over-lubrication. This is a means of ascertaining whether the engine is working with the right pressure of oil. It is essential that the cylinders should not run short of oil, but too much oil will clog the plugs, cause smoke in the exhaust, and will eventually cause pre-ignition through excessive carbon deposit in the cylinders. (See p. 134.)

A sooty deposit, especially noticeable on the ignition plugs, is a sign of strong mixture. (See p. 134.)

4. Grinding Valves.

Do not touch the valves unless the compression is poor.

The inlet and exhaust valves, however, especially the latter, may require re-grinding occasionally. Experience

Fig. 90.
TAKING OFF VALVE COVER TO INSPECT CYLINDER.

would indicate that an examination should be made every 5,000 miles, the compressions being tested as indicated under two "compressions" (when testing a cylinder see that the plugs in short cylinder are air-tight). If each of the cylinders shows that it will hold its compression well, then the valves must be in good order, if not, then the exhaust valve should be taken out and examined.

Having ascertained which is the cylinder with poor compression, the valves of that cylinder should be ground in. This should be done *gently* and lightly with a large screwdriver, and *not* with a brace ; the finest emery powder (with emery flour to finish up with) should be used, mixed with oil. Do not use coarse emery. To get at the valves take off the bridges holding the exhaust chamber on (Fig. 91) and the pipe union underneath, then remove the exhaust chamber (Fig. 92) ; take off valve covers (Fig. 90) ; take out the valve cotter by lifting spring (with valve lifter) at the same time holding down the valve from the top ; then push up valve and withdraw as shown in Fig. 94.

FIG. 91.
UNSCREWING EXHAUST PIPE BRIDGES.

FIG. 92.
REMOVING PRIMARY EXHAUST CHAMBER.

Do not continue grinding a valve till it is dry, i.e., till a bright ring is formed on the face of the valve (before it is wiped), but raise the valve and turn it to another position after every few grindings, occasionally wiping the valve clean and applying fresh oil and emery.

77

It is more economical to grind valves a little and often rather than to allow them to get into bad condition.

FIG. 93.
REMOVING VALVE COVER TO GET AT VALVE.

FIG. 94.
WITHDRAWING VALVE.

5. Tappets.

In all cases when the valves have been " ground in," or changed for any reason, attention should be paid to the tappets.

These should be adjusted so that the clearance between the fibre and the valve spindle is about ·01 in. for the exhaust and ·005 in. for the inlet valve. The valve should, of course, be closed, and the tappet not lifted by the cam, when this is being done. A feeler gauge may

78

be used as shown inserted at A in Fig. 95. A special gauge is now supplied with every new Rolls-Royce car.

CAUTION.

The cams are made so that the timing of the valves is correct when the slackness is only just enough to ensure the valves closing properly. In checking and unchecking the screw provided for this adjustment, care should be taken that two spanners are used in such a way that one resists the turning exerted by the other (as in Fig. 95), otherwise if great force is used the pin which prevents the tappet turning may be damaged.

NOTE.—In chassis numbered higher than (about) 750, the tappets may be set thus :—Take all the slack out by the screw adjustment, then, to set to correct amount of slack, screw the screw into its socket one-sixth of a turn (counted by the

FIG. 95.
LOCKING THE TAPPET ADJUSTMENT. A SHOWS FEEL GAUGE IN USE.

hexagon head) and check the nut, when the correct amount of slack will be obtained, because the pitch of the screw is 20 threads per inch, or ·05 inch per thread, which divided by six, equals ·008 inch of slackness. This is a good average amount for both inlet and exhaust.

6. Pressure Feed.

Fig. 96 shows pressure feed regulator D in position ; A is the steel pipe leading from the exhaust box ; B is the pipe from the hand pump and C the pipe to the petrol tank. For the periodical cleaning, it should only be necessary

to take the top off, removing the three screws ; the two small valves should then be taken out and cleaned with paraffin, and the gauze cleaned with a brush.

Fig. 97 shows the pressure feed regulator taken entirely to pieces :—A is top half, B bottom half, joined together by

FIG. 96.
PRESSURE FEED REGULATOR IN POSITION.

four screws as M, with gauze filter F and fibre joint E in between them. When putting together, the non-return valve H (with fluted stem) goes on the seating N, then put spring K (the weaker one) in body D and fix the latter,

FIG. 97.
PRESSURE FEED REGULATOR IN PIECES.

thereby compressing K ; then the safety valve G fits on to D, with the (stronger) spring J on top of G ; and, finally, the cover C is attached, with three screws to it, which should be screwed up evenly.

BRAKES.

7. Foot Brake.

To adjust the central brake, screw up the star nut (B, Fig. 98), which is situated underneath the lower brake shoe on the near side. This can be done by withdrawing the spring locking bolt or trigger A in Fig. 98 (no tools required). Do not shorten the pull rod. The brake should "come on"

FIG. 98.
UNLOCKING AND ADJUSTING STAR NUT.

FIG. 99.
SET SCREW A FOR TOP SHOE.

when the foot pedal is half stroke down. If the lower shoe rubs on the brake drum when the brake is in the "off" position, the top shoe must be brought nearer by screwing down the set screw (A in Fig. 99), which is in the bracket

fixed to the cross-member of the frame. Screw down the top shoe until it clears the drum by $\frac{1}{64}$th of an inch afterwards checking the screw by means of the lock nut.

N.B.—Remember that the foot brake necessarily expands with heat, and if it is set too close it may not be sufficiently clear in its "off" position after a long downhill run.

8. Side Brakes.

To adjust the rear brakes, take off the cover which protects the brakes (Fig. 100). This cover is made in two halves, and can be easily removed by taking off the five nuts which secure it. The brake shoes are connected together by two eye-bolts and a turnbuckle (B in Fig. 101). Slack back the two check nuts (A A in Fig. 101) (one right and one left-hand thread) and expand the shoes by screwing round the

FIG. 100.
SHOWING COVER REMOVED.

turnbuckle until the shoes touch the brake drum, and the lever (G in Fig. 101), to which the wire rope is connected touches the rear axle. Now slack back the turnbuckle until the end of the lever G has $1\frac{1}{8}$ in. of movement before the shoes are hard on the drum. Check the turnbuckle by the two lock-nuts. Then adjust the stops (C C in Fig. 101), one of which will be found behind each brake shoe. Slack the bolts which secure these stops and slide the *rear* one, C, along until it leaves $\frac{1}{64}$ in. of clearance between the brake drum and rear shoe. Tighten up in this position. Then slide the forward stop along until it forces the forward brake shoe slightly outward, so as to bring the operating lever $\frac{1}{16}$ in. away from the axle (A in

Fig. 102), and tighten up in this position. After adjusting both brakes in this manner, the wire compensating rope may require adjusting. This can be done by means of a turnbuckle (F in Fig. 101) which is on the off side of the chassis.

FIG. 101.
BRAKE ADJUSTED CORRECTLY.
TURNBUCKLE B, CHECK NUTS A, LEVER G, STOPS C, TURNBUCKLE F.

FIG. 102.
CORRECT CLEARANCE AT A, $\frac{1}{16}$ INCH WITH BRAKE OFF.

Fig. 101 shows brake correctly adjusted ; Fig. 103 shows bad position of brake, i.e., requiring adjustment.

NOTE.—In adjusting all brakes care should be taken to make the adjustments at those points in the mechanism intended by us for adjustment and not at any other part, otherwise the various parts might not remain in their correct relative positions. The means of adjustment are as near as possible to the worn part, viz., on the screwed rods which connect the two halves of the brake shoes. It may be found necessary at some time to replace the wire rope on the rear brakes. It is necessary when doing this to see that it is secured at the correct length. The adjustment must be such that, when the hand lever is in the " off " position, the wire rope has *no slack* in it but is long enough for the levers to which it is attached to be *both right back* against the back axle. No other length of wire rope is correct except as a temporary means of adjustment.

FIG. 103.
INCORRECT ADJUSTMENT OF BRAKE WHEN "OFF."

9. Steering Gear.

At regular intervals this should be examined, particularly to see that the steering horns are tightly attached to the stub axles, and that all bolts are secured with nuts and split pins, especially noticing that the nuts are tight and that the split pins are not nearly worn through owing to a loose nut rubbing against them. The ball ends of the cross steering rods can be adjusted when slack in the same manner as the torque and radius rods described in next paragraph.

Torque and Radius Rods.

Should the under-part of the car rattle badly on rough roads the above rods should be examined. In the 1908-9 cars provision has been made to enable the slack to be taken out of the ball fittings (at both ends) by slacking the check nuts and screwing up the set screws (which will be found on the extreme ends of the tubes) tightly, then turning back ⅛th of a turn (to allow free working), and re-tightening the check nuts (see Fig. 104). There are *nine* of these ball-end fittings including the cross-steering rod ends.

FIG. 104.

HOW TO ADJUST BALL-END FITTINGS SUCH AS ON CROSS STEERING ROD, TORQUE RODS AND RADIUS RODS (9 IN ALL).

Spring Clips.

The clips which fasten the axles on to the springs should not be allowed to work loose.

10. Petrol Filters.

FIG. 105.
MAIN PETROL FILTER IN POSITION.

FIG. 106.

MAIN PETROL FILTER IN PIECES FOR CLEANING.

11 & 12. Filter.

D in Fig. 107 shows petrol filter at the opening or filling hole of the tank; when dismantling this and replacing, put an even pressure on every screw by screwing each screw a little at a time in the order shown in Fig. 108; when these locking screws have been loosed one turn in the order shown in Fig. 108, the cover will unscrew either by hand or with the back-axle tool E in Fig. 109, while the cover of the tank is off and the filter out, clean the bottom of the tank with a cloth (not cotton waste); the bottom should be free from grit and globules of water.

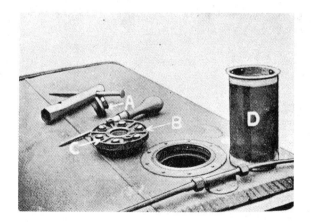

FIG. 107.
PETROL STRAINER AND FITTINGS.

FIG. 108.
SHOWING ORDER OF SCREWING AND UNSCREWING LOCKING
SCREWS (TURN EACH A LITTLE AT A TIME).

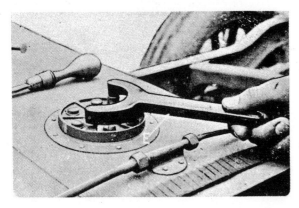

FIG. 109.
THE BACK AXLE TOOL E FITS THE COVER (THE LOCKING
SCREWS MUST BE LOOSENED BEFORE UNSCREWING COVER).

13. Carburettor.

FIG. 110.
TAKING OFF COVER OF FLOAT CHAMBER.

FIG. 111.
FLOAT AND FLOAT FEED VALVE REMOVED FOR CLEANING.
(See that the float has not any petrol inside it.)

14. Loose Nuts.

Place the car over a convenient pit and let a careful, skilled mechanic examine and test every nut, bolt and pin throughout the car in order to tighten up every one that has loosened at all.

APPENDIX IV.

EVERY 20,000 MILES OR TWO YEARS.

It is recommended as the safest and most economical course to send a car to its makers for dismantlement and report at least once every 20,000 miles.

Should this be quite impossible, it is most important to see that any overhaul is thoroughly well done by competent people who have the necessary skilled labour, proper appliances, and special steels.

Should any of the pistons, piston pins, or connecting rods be taken apart at any time, care should be taken, when putting them together, to see that the oil hole in the bronze bush of the small end of the connecting rod is on the *opposite* side to the hole in the piston pin, otherwise the oil will be forced straight through and will flood the cylinders (causing excessive smoking), even with the oil pressure set to its lowest.

APPENDIX V.

INSTRUCTIONS FOR STARTING, STOPPING, ETC.

SUPPLIES.

Before starting at the beginning of a day or after a stop, see that there is a sufficient supply of petrol, oil and water in the tanks, some spare tyres and inner tubes (in good condition), a complete equipment of tools and spare parts.

FILLING WITH WATER.

The radiator should not be filled higher than two inches above the tops of the tubes, and the level should not be allowed to get much below this. The **Level.** white line in Fig. 112 shows the correct level. If there is less than $3\frac{1}{2}$ inches between the top of the water and the top af the filter, the water will sometimes spray out through the cap as though it were boiling.

FIG. 112.

FILL UP TO LEVEL OF WHITE LINE.

When adding water to the radiator see that no straw or leaves, etc., are poured in. Use only soft water (preferably rain water).

Incrustation. A teaspoonful of "Incrusto" per gallon of water may be added to prevent scale and rust. This preparation is obtainable from the Anglo-Bosphorous Oil Co., Ltd., Bristol (mention for ROLLS-ROYCE car).

FILLING WITH PETROL.

Petrol should only be poured into the petrol tank through a very fine wire gauze strainer — fine enough to stop water. Funnels wet with water must

Strainer. not be used for replenishing petrol tanks.

For filling, it is only necessary to unscrew cap A (Fig. 113) with the box key shown.

FIG. 113.
FILLING PLUG A AND KEY.

FIG. 114.
THE CORRECT WAY TO HOLD A "SHELL" PETROL-CAN SO AS TO ALLOW A FREE INTAKE OF AIR AND A CLEAN FLOW OF PETROL.

The R-R carburettors are regulated for "Shell" spirit, having an average specific gravity of ·710 ; when the car is taken abroad a slight alteration to the

Density. jets may be necessary to suit the foreign petrol, but this should be obtainable with the small lever on dashboard (see " Carburettor ").

If the density varies greatly from the standard (·710), the float may require adjusting, *i.e.*, add weight (*e.g.*, a washer), for heavier spirit, and *vice versa*.

N.B.—When touring in France do not ask for or accept "Petrole," which is frequently advertised outside stores, for this means "paraffin" ; the French word

Foreign Spirit. for petrol is "essence," and the best known brands in that country are " Motricine," " Stelline," and " Motonaphta."

FILLING WITH OIL.

Open the overflow cock A (Fig. 115) to see if oil runs out do not be deceived by a small amount that may be in the cock itself) ; if none flows out, turn on the supply cock B (in the direction of the pipe) until oil commences to flow out of

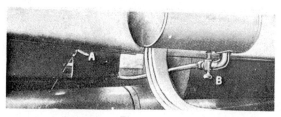

Fig. 115.
OVERFLOW COCK A OPEN, SUPPLY COCK B OPEN (PARALLEL TO PIPE).

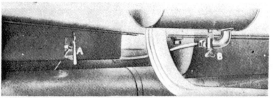

FIG. 116.
OVERFLOW COCK A CLOSED, SUPPLY COCK B CLOSED (AT RIGHT ANGLES TO PIPE).

the overflow cock (the car being level), then close both cocks as in Fig. 116, and refill the reserve tank with engine oil (Fig. 117).

(See Appendix VI., p. 108 on "Lubrication" as to right sort of oil to use.)

FIG. 117.

REFILLING SUPPLY TANK WITH OIL.

NOTE.—In this chapter it is presumed that the general ubrication of the car has been properly attended to.

STARTING THE ENGINE.

See that gear lever is in neutral position (A in Fig. 118) and brake on. Turn on petrol tap vertically, as in Fig. 119. If the petrol in the tank is low it may be necessary to give the hand pump (Fig. 120) a few strokes till the gauge (left hand one) shows *some* pressure. The carburettor may be slightly flooded by gently pressing down the float (A in Fig. 121) until the petrol begins to run out at the top of the float-feed (avoid "joggling" the float, as this is apt in time to knock a hole in it), the ignition control lever must be pushed *right back* to the "late" position (*i.e.*, fully retarded), and the throttle partly opened by moving the governor control lever one-third up the quadrant, then both ignitions switched on. Fig. 120 shows correct position of levers on steering wheel for starting engine.

93

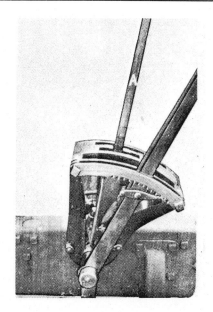

FIG. 118

GEAR LEVER **A** IN **NEUTRAL** POSITION.

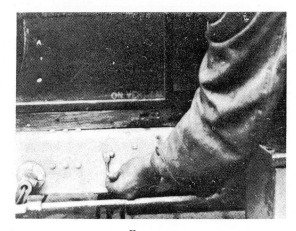

FIG. 119.

PETROL TAP IN THE "ON" POSITION.

94

N.B.—Severe injury to the person turning the starting-handle may result if the ignition be not kept in the "late" position while the current is switched on.

FIG. 120.

GIVING HAND PUMP A FEW STROKES.

(NOTE POSITION OF CONTROL LEVERS.)

FIG. 121.

PRESS A TO "FLOOD" CARBURETTOR.

The engine should then start with a few half-turns of the starting-handle. When starting the engine always pull the handle upwards; do not push down; *i.e.*, the handle

should rest on the four fingers (Fig. 121); if it is "gripped" it might cause injury to the wrist or arm in the event of a "back-fire." On a cold morning, should there be any trouble in starting the engine, about half an egg-cupful of

FIG. 122.

HOW TO HOLD THE STARTING HANDLE.

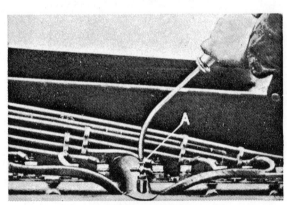

FIG. 123.

INJECT A LITTLE PETROL AT A IF NECESSARY.

petrol may be injected into the induction pipe through the small tap A (Fig. 123); beware of injecting *too much*, and re-member to shut the tap again (vertical position). (If, however, this were adopted as a regular practice when not necessary, it would cause "dirty" cylinders). The pouring of some hot water over the carburettor and induction pipe will also facilitate starting. The stiffness of the engine when first turning in cold weather is due to the heavy viscosity of the oil at low temperatures, and may be reduced by filling the radiator with hot water.

As soon as the engine starts, the ignition should be moderately advanced and the throttle gradually closed (by means of the governor lever) until the engine runs at a slow speed ; the levers on the steering wheel will then probably be in the position shown in Fig. 124. The battery ignition may afterwards be switched off, if desired.

The jet regulator on dashboard may be put towards the "strong" position until the engine is warm, when it should be moved back to the *weakest* position that will give satisfactory running.

FIG. 124.
POSITION OF LEVERS WITH ENGINE RUNNING.

Care should be taken to see that the pressure gauge on the dashboard (right hand side) shows that the oil is circulating properly.

The engine should be allowed to run for a few minutes till the carburettor has warmed up before attempting to make the engine "pull" well or run regularly at slow speeds.

The engine should always be run with the ignition advanced as far as possible, but not far enough to cause a squeaking or knocking at the pistons or a decrease of power. Retard the ignition as the speed of the engine decreases.

For normal running, set the engine (as in Fig 124) to run slowly by the hand regulator (marked "Governor"), and accelerate as required by the accelerator pedal.

APPENDIX VI.

LUBRICATION OF ENGINE.

NOTE.—In dealing with the Lubrication of the Engine, in order to make this chapter complete in itself, there is necessarily a considerable amount of repetition, both of instructions and of illustrations, which have appeared in previous chapters.

General.
Attention to Details.
Over-lubricate rather than under-lubricate, and pay special attention to details. It is curious how often we find on examining a client's car that although the engine, main bearings, etc., have been well looked after, some apparently unimportant parts, where but slight movement takes place, have been entirely neglected.

Oil or Grease.
Grease should never be used except in the grease cups, as it clogs the special channels and ducts intended for the flow of oil.

Gear Oil.
For the gear-boxes and most moving parts *other than the engine*, best thick gear oil should be used ; it should have good lubricating properties and have a very heavy body, but must be sufficiently fluid to run slowly even in cold weather.

Good gear oil can be obtained from Price's Patent Candle Co., London and Liverpool, and from the Dee Oil Co., Ltd., of Saltney, near Chester (mention that it is for the ROLLS-ROYCE car).

Engine Oil.
Great care must be taken to use only the correct kind of oil in the ROLLS-ROYCE *engine*. A mineral oil of good lubricating properties and body is needed, with a small percentage of suitable fatty oil which will neither become oxidized or acid. Oil suitable for the ROLLS-ROYCE engines can be obtained from us or from any of the following firms :—Price's Patent Candle Co., Ltd., of London and Liverpool (we recommend Price's Motorine B for summer use and Motorine C for winter use, but give preference to B whenever it will circulate freely) ; the Dee Oil Co., Ltd., Saltney, near Chester ; and J. C. & J. Field, Ltd., Upper Marsh, Lambeth, London. When ordering from the two latter firms ask for their Compound Motor Cylinder Oil suitable for ROLLS-

ROYCE engines. When buying oil on the road it is important to see that it is delivered in the makers' original tins.

When touring on the Continent, be sure to get a thick motor oil; the ordinary motor oils there sold are often too thin for our engines. It is best to take a liberal supply of the right oil from home, but if compelled to purchase on the road, we believe "Huile D F," made by Desmarais Frères (which can be found in most provincial towns of France), will be found fairly good. It is slightly thicker than Price's Motorine B or C, and may, therefore, require to be heated for use.

In the ROLLS-ROYCE engine the old form of lubrication by "splash" has been superseded, and a far more perfect system introduced, by means of which **Engine.** the correct lubrication of every part is ensured at all times, including those surfaces which in a petrol engine are subject to enormous pressures at the moment of explosion.

FIG. 130.
OVERFLOW COCK CLOSED.

Attached to the bottom of the crank-chamber is a well or "sump" holding about one gallon of oil. On the right-hand side of the engine, underneath the commutator, is a small gear pump which revolves with the engine; this pump draws oil from the well (through a filter fitted therein), and sends it into the three main bearings of the crankshaft; the crankshaft is hollow, and the oil being under a considerable pressure, enters the crankshaft through holes at these three points, it is then driven along the interior of the crankshaft to feed the other smaller bearings of the shaft (in the ROLLS-ROYCE there is a bearing on each side of every crank), and it also flows out of the shaft at the six crank pins (through suitable outlets), thus lubricating the "big ends" of the connecting rods, whence it travels up the connecting rods to the gudgeon pins, pistons and cylinder

walls, eventually draining back to the oil well, and so providing perfect lubrication.

The correct level of oil in the well is important, and is indicated by a special overflow cock (D Fig. 136) fixed on the lower half of the crank-chamber, in rear of the oil-well;

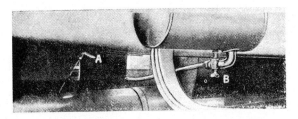

FIG. 131.
OVERFLOW COCK OPEN.

this cock is operated by a small lever which will be found fixed to the chassis frame below a brass tank on the left side of the car (A in Fig. 130); it is closed when the lever is vertical (A in Fig. 130). This overflow cock indicates the normal

FIG. 132.
REFILLING OIL TANK.

height of the oil when the car is *level;* the oil when the engine is still should not be filled in above this level, otherwise it would be disastrous when mounting hills, and it should not be allowed to get *much below* this level or the pump would fail to properly keep up the circulation.

The overflow-cock should be opened daily (A in Fig. 131) to see if oil runs out (do not be deceived by a small amount of oil which may be in the cock itself) ; if the cock is free from dirt and no oil flows out, the level is getting low and more oil is required in the well.

There will be seen a brass cylindrical reservoir on the left side of the car, attached to the chassis frame (Fig. 132) : this is a reserve tank of oil from which the oil-well of the engine can be replenished, it should therefore be kept full with the correct sort of engine oil ; to let oil from this tank into the well, turn on the tap of the tank (B in Fig. 131)

THE ENGINE OIL PUMP.
FIG. 133.

(this tap is closed when at right-angles to the pipe) ; the overflow-cock should be kept open while the oil is flowing in, and the tap of the supply tank turned off (B in Fig. 130) as soon as it commences to run out at the overflow (the car should be level or this will not be a true indication). A good practice is to fill up to the overflow before starting out, and then every 100 to 200 miles let in some oil from the supply tank till it runs out of the overflow, but do not forget to shut the overflow-cock again, as well as the supply tap of the tank before starting off.

The correct amount of oil contained by the oil-well of the engine is the same as that contained in the supply tank, viz., approximately one gallon.

NOTE.—When the tap of the supply tank is turned on, the oil flows into the well of the engine *very slowly.*

The engine should be oil-retaining, *i.e.,* there should be practically no waste or leakage noticeable. Any serious leak of oil should be attended to.

Notwithstanding the correct quantity of oil having been put into the engine, the driver must always be certain that the oil is *circulating* properly, otherwise (unlike " splash " lubrication) the oil in the well would be useless, for it would not reach the cranks. The proper circulation of the oil is denoted by the pressure gauge situated on the right-hand side of the dashboard, above the switches.

FIG. 134.

When the engine is running, this gauge should never indicate less than 3 lbs. or more than 20 lbs. per square inch.

The oil pump (Fig. 133) is provided with an automatic " by-pass " or relief valve which governs the maximum pressure at which the pump circulates the oil ; to alter this relief valve—and so adjust the pressure at which the oil should constantly circulate—there will be found a large screw (A) just underneath the relief valve, checked by a lock-nut (B) ; this screw should be screwed up or down as the pressure is required to be increased or diminished ; when making this adjustment, have the engine running and watch the gauge.

Fig. 134 shows the pump in pieces, relief valve C, valve seat B, valve spring K, fibre washer E, screwed collar F, square steel driving tube J, suction side S, delivery side D, body of pump A, adjusting screw G, and lock-nut H

Fig. 135 shows how the pump should be fixed when in position ; D is the delivery side (front of engine) ; S the suction side leading to base chamber ; the arrow marks the direction of rotation.

Do not cut the oil circulation pressure down low, but run with it as high as you can *without* causing smoke in the exhaust ; there *should be* a slight smoke visible in the

FIG. 135.

exhaust when first starting up the engine from cold, but there is something wrong if the exhaust *continuously* emits blue smoke with the oil pressure set below 7 lbs.

If the gauge shows signs of dropping back, the oil feed is failing and should at once be attended to (try letting more oil into the engine) ; if the gauge drops to *zero* the car must on no account be driven on (except in emergencies for a mile or two) otherwise the white-metal bearings may be destroyed.

NOTE.—It is advisable, for much night work, to fit a small electric lamp over or behind the pressure gauge, with a press-button switch against the driver's seat.

The needle of the pressure gauge should be constant and should not vary more than 2 or 3 lbs. for *any* engine speed.

Causes of Engine Lubrication Failure.

If the gauge begins to fluctuate considerably, or the oil pressure fails completely when the engine is running, the following are the probable causes :—

(1) Insufficient oil in the well of the engine (as already dealt with).

FIG. 136.

OIL FILTER AND SUCTION PIPE TAKEN APART.

(2) The filter or one of the oil pipes is choked up. This filter is situated in the oil-well : the cover of the oil-well (A, Fig. 136) should be taken down as instructed (p. 55) and cleaned, together with the filter (B, Fig. 136) and suction pipe (C, Fig. 136) leading to the oil-pump, then replace filter in the well and refix the well, taking care to make a good joint (with good stout paper) on to the crank-chamber ; see also that the unions of the oil pipes are screwed up tight, then refill the well with a *fresh* charge of oil from the side tank up to the overflow level ; if preferred, the port G in Fig. 66 (p. 56) may be used for refilling, to save time.

(3) The relief valve on the oil-pump is being held open by some foreign substance deposited on the face; this valve can be easily taken out and cleaned.

(4) There is a leak somewhere in the oil system, probably in one of the pipes or unions. If the leak is on the "delivery" side of the pump it will reveal itself by a slight flow of oil; but if it is on the "suction" side, the pump will be drawing in air, and the location of the leak will not be so easy; the short suction pipe (C, Fig. 136) between the oil-well and the pump might be taken off and blown through to see if it is split anywhere or the soldering of the unions has cracked. A hole so small as not to be detected by blowing may yet be sufficient to cause the gauge to register zero.

(5) The oil system wants "priming" owing to some part having been recently dismantled.

FIG. 137.
"PRIMING" OIL CIRCULATION.

Whenever the oil-well, pipes, or pump are taken down for any purpose and put back again, special care should be taken when first starting the engine up (after refilling) to see that the pressure gauge reads correctly, for an "air lock" may form which will prevent the flow of oil; should this occur the pipes should be "primed," by unscrewing one of the unions leading from the trunk pipe to the crankshaft, or the special plug (Fig. 137) provided in some types, and injecting oil therein by means of the oil-syringe, or it may be poured in from an oil-can (with patience). The unions can then be refixed and the engine started up again, but it is possible that a second attempt will be required.

APPENDIX VII.

CARE OF CLUTCH.

The clutch is normally oil-retaining, but at high speeds a certain amount may leak away; therefore, if the clutch becomes "too fierce," a small quantity **Clutch.** (say an egg-cupful) of engine oil should be fed with a syringe on to the surface, as shown in Fig. 138 (the clutch pedal being depressed), to make it work smoothly.

FIG. 138.
OILING CLUTCH SURFACE.

Too much oil will cause the clutch to slip; if this occurs, *i.e.*, if the engine can be made to race when the clutch is engaged and in trying to drive the car, the car should immediately be stopped and the surplus oil let out through the plug A by taking this off and running the engine, or drawn out by means of a syringe, as shown in Fig. 139.

N.B.—If the car is driven on with the clutch slipping, the leather will soon be burnt and destroyed, which will necessitate dismantling and re-leathering the clutch.

An over-oiled clutch will also make changing gear difficult, especially when starting the car from " rest," for, with the clutch pedal depressed, the gears will not engage, as the clutch will not readily stop revolving on account of the film

FIG. 139.
SHOWING OIL DRAIN A AND ALTERNATIVE METHOD OF WITHDRAWING SURPLUS OIL.

of oil between the leather and the flywheel which prevents the clutch from disengaging properly when the clutch pedal is depressed.

Should the clutch become over-oiled, though none has been applied by hand, it will probably be caused by leakage through the small valve on the end of the crankshaft. This valve, which is opened when the clutch pedal is fully depressed, allows oil from the crankshaft to feed the spigot or clutch bearing. The valve may have stuck or may not close properly, owing to some foreign substance getting underneath the seat. The spindle which actuates the valve will be seen (B, in Fig. 140) projecting from the end of the clutch shaft (by taking off the coupling).

This spindle moves with the clutch and is held in position by a grub screw (A, in Fig. 140), which passes through the driving pin on which the square blocks are fitted. By unscrewing this grub screw the spindle is free to move endways, and if pushed in towards the engine will be found to come against a

FIG. 140.

surface which gives to further pressure. This is the valve which opens when pressed but is closed by means of a spring when pressure is released. This is a means of ascertaining if the valve has stuck. This action is, of course, carried on in a

FIG. 141.

similar manner by depressing the clutch when the spindle is held in position with the grub screw. To set this spindle, the clutch should be engaged and the spindle brought into position so as just to touch the valve (but not to open it). It should then be brought back $\frac{1}{18}$ in., and locked by means of the grub screw. This is the normal position, and should be increased or reduced as found suitable.

Fig. 141 shows the parts of this device; the spring E should be inserted (large end first) after the plug A; fix valve B in seating C, and screw bodily into end of spigot.

Should there be anything wrong with the valve it can be taken out and cleaned by dismantling the clutch. *Before* putting the clutch together, the engine should be run with the

FIG. 142.

OIL VALVE IN PLACE.

valve in place (Fig. 142) to test if the valve really shuts off the oil, *i.e.*, whether it is properly ground to an oil-tight joint. There is also a tight worsted plug (A Fig. 141) fitted at the crankshaft extension to prevent a too free supply of oil from flowing to the clutch, and to act as a filter to the oil. This plug should be as tight a fit as possible.

Care must be taken that the joint made between the valve seating and the end of the clutch spigot is oil-tight.

Note that the above oiling device is for oiling the clutch bearing only, not the clutch itself.

For lubricating clutch-operating mechanism, see p. 42. Appendix. I.

RESUME.

Should a "slipping" clutch be experienced at any time, the following are the probable causes :—

(a) Too much oil (which can be drawn out with syringe (Fig. 139) or by removing the special plug (A in Fig. 139), in the flywheel, and running the engine for a while).

(b) The parts have worn out of adjustment, resulting in the pedal lever catching the floor board or other mechanism, having got to the limit of its stroke. This can be adjusted

FIG. 143.

CLEARANCE A FOR CLUTCH PAD.

by shortening the link which is situated at the top end of the vertical levers, giving it a few complete turns. In case the fault cannot be remedied at the time, it is advisable to *change on to a lower gear* until the clutch cools or a place is reached where the necessary adjustment can be made.

(c) The clutch leather having worn until the coupling has no end-play, resulting in the coupling preventing the clutch spring forcing the clutch into the conical portion of the flywheel.

N.B.—It is most essential not to run the car with the clutch slipping, but to stop and attend to the fault *at once*, otherwise the leather may quickly be destroyed.

CLUTCH PAD.

There is a small brake in the form of a fibre pad against which the clutch rubs when depressed. The object of this brake is to stop the clutch from revolving, and so facilitate the changing of gears; it may at times require adjusting, *i.e.*, bringing nearer to the flange of the clutch on which it rubs. It can be moved along the underframe by unscrewing the bolts by which it is attached (the holes being elongated). This brake should be adjusted so that, when the clutch is "in," the fibre should be about $\frac{1}{32}$ in. off the flange (A in Fig. 143).

APPENDIX VIII.

IGNITION.

NOTE.—In order to make this chapter complete in itself, there is necessarily some repetition of instructions and illustrations which appear in previous chapters.

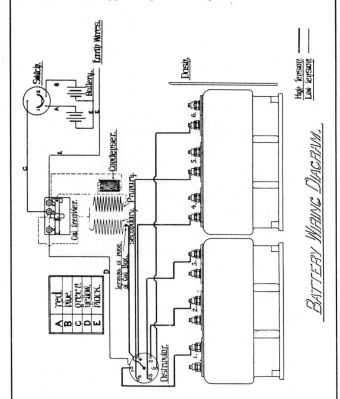

FIG. 144.

The battery ignition is useful for—

1. Starting the engine (when it is preferable to have both switched on).
2. For slow running in traffic.
3. Re-starting on the switch.
4. Investigating when anything is wrong.

Outside these requirements the magneto is the better ignition.

Figs. 144 and 145 show the wiring of the battery and magneto ignitions respectively.

The most frequent trouble with ignition is found in the plugs. This generally only affects one cylinder at a time, and, therefore, gives bad ignition generally

Plugs. (not always) at regular intervals, and *before* upsetting any other part of the ignition, which is probably working well, the defective plug should be changed and carefully tested.

In order to discover which plug, if any, is missing fire :—

(a) Switch off the current and feel the sparking plugs to

FIG. 146.
SHORT CIRCUITING A SPARKING PLUG AT A.

ascertain if one is colder than the others. This would indicate that it had been missing fire. Or, if this method of detection fails :—

(b) "Short-circuit" each sparking plug in succession by connecting it by means of a screw-driver to some convenient metal work on the engine (Fig. 146); if the plug has been firing properly this "short-circuiting" will reduce the speed of the engine by reason of the additional "mis-firing" thus caused; if it does not, then the plug being tested is probably the faulty one and should be changed for another one known to be good (and clean) which should always be carried in readiness on the car.

Having discovered that a plug is at fault :—

(a) Slip off the wire (Fig. 64), screw out the plug with special key provided, and examine the gap between the points. When setting the gaps it is best to fix the magneto plugs at ·01 inch and the battery plugs at ·02 inch, to allow for the points burning apart. All plugs of the same ignition should have equal gaps. Rolls-Royce, Ltd., now supply a special gauge with each new car.

If the gap is right :—

(b) See if the points are coated with oil; this will insulate them so effectively that the spark cannot jump from one point to another; they are best cleaned by soaking the plug in petrol (about half-an-inch depth).

FIG. 147.
PULLING OUT HIGH-TENSION WIRES.

(c) The insulation may be coated with carbon either from too rich a mixture or from burnt oil in the cylinders, this will cause the current to flow quietly across without firing the charge. Secondly the insulation may be cracked or otherwise faulty either on the outside of the plug or within the construction of the plug itself; and thirdly, the insulation may be wet.

If there should be "missing fire" with the battery ignition and the plugs are not at fault, the commutator and distributor should be looked at and

Missing Fire. carefully cleaned, *especially the internal face of the distributor ring*, on which the carbon brush rubs. This should be cleaned with a dry rag. See that the contacts are working properly. (See p. 69.)

It will be remembered that the following figures show how to get at the distributor and commutator of the battery ignition, for their periodical cleaning, etc. :—

FIG. 148.

LIFTING OFF THE TWO CLIPS.

FIG. 149.

REMOVING HIGH-TENSION COVER.

Should the failure still continue on the battery ignition,

(a) The usual signs that the mixture is too weak for the battery ignition are irregular firing or failure to fire at some particular speed (at which the carburation is weakest). These failures can generally be improved by advancing the ignition.

b) When you are satisfied that this is not the cause of the failure, then examine the terminals at which the wires make contact with the accumulators, and see that the screws are firmly screwed down, and the wires making good contact. Trace the wires through the whole electric system, especially the low-tension (the smaller

FIG. 152.

REMOVING SIDE COVER.

of the two sets of) wires, to see that there are no loose connections or fractures.

(c) Test the accumulators with a voltmeter ; each cell should record not less than two volts. A cell will work as low as 1·8, but they should not be allowed to run lower than 1·9 volts each. If there is any doubt as to the condition of the accumulators, make this test before proceeding with the tests above enumerated.

(d) Not until you have gone through the whole of the above tests should the trembler on the coil be touched. If one of the platinum points is deeply pitted, and the other point has assumed the shape of a cone to fit into the pit, both points should be filed with a very fine file until they are flat. In order to adjust a trembler, follow carefully the printed instructions inside the lid of the coil-box. The coil or *trembler should not be touched* until you are sure that everything else in the ignition system is all right, as in doing so the trouble is often made worse. To get the tremblers into the best working condition is a delicate operation, and therefore the tremblers should

FIG. 153.
CONTACT BREAKER EXPOSED, AND GAUGE.

not be unnecessarily disturbed. (See "Coil Trembler," page 136.)

N.B.—In any case, do not pull the trembler to pieces until you have opened it with your finger and have seen that the points are really in bad contact or out of adjustment.

If the "missing fire" is sometimes on all the cylinders and on both ignitions, then it is almost certainly a question of carburation (which is treated under the heading

of "Carburation"), but should this failure take place with the magneto ignition, the low tension contact breaker on the magneto should be examined carefully (Fig. 153) to see that

FIG. 154.
TAKING OUT MAGNETO.

the small lever carrying the platinum point is working *freely*, and that the platinum points are in good order and correctly set. The small round cap must of course be slipped off

FIG. 155.
UNSCREWING EXHAUST PIPE BRIDGES.

first. This setting is correct when the break is the amount equal to the thickness of the gauge on the special magneto spanner (shown in Fig. 153).

(It is good practice to carry a spare contact breaker for the magneto.)

If all these are found in good order, the earth wire, which leads to the switch intended to stop the ignition, should be examined, and can best be tested by disconnecting it entirely from the magneto, stopping the engine when desired by the throttle. If this does not locate the fault then it may be something more serious inside the magneto, which should be taken off (Fig. 154) and sent to someone well versed in its construction.

FIG. 156.

REMOVING EXHAUST PIPES.

When taking magneto off, first remove exhaust chamber (Figs. 155 and 156), pull out the wires, loosen and swing back the bridge piece. (See note on page 135 as to putting it back rightly.)

The high-tension distributor of the magneto should be taken to pieces periodically as already instructed (Appendix II., Fig. 87, p. 69) and the convenient parts removed and thoroughly cleaned. Fig. 157 shows the cover of the magneto distributor removed. Any defect with the distributor is generally manifest by pre-ignitions, whereas if the defect is with the low-tension contact breaker, it is manifest by misfires. When replacing the wires on the distributor of magneto, see that the number of rings cut in the ebonite of each terminal corresponds with the figure beside each hole.

RE-SETTING THE IGNITION.

When an engine does not pick up quickly and sweetly from slow speeds, it may be due to the ignition being too early, and if bringing the ignition to a late position does not cure it, the magneto, if firing too early, should be adjusted relatively later than the engine.

Magneto Ignition.

A collar (F in Fig. 158) with three screws in it has been provided on the driving shaft to enable this to be done. These screws (one usually suffices) should be slackened slightly and it will be found that a large nail or similar object can be put in the hollow pin of the coupling, and the magneto turned in the required direction. When this is done, the three screws in the collar should be firmly tightened.

FIG. 158.

COLLAR F, FOR TIMING MAGNETO.

Especial care must be taken that the high-tension distributor is making contact with the No. 1 distributing plate when the No. 1 (front) piston is in the firing position. Then exact timing can be attained by observing the *exact* moment that the low-tension platinum points break contact, which should be when the piston is exactly in the highest position on the firing stroke, at the same time the mark on the flywheel (corresponding to the crank pin), will be in the central top position.

If it is found necessary at any time to remove the magneto, take care to put it back with the universal joints together at the same half-turn and the correct relative revolution. There is only one correct relation for every six positions. Also see that the number of circles cut in the ebonite of each terminal corresponds with the figure marked at each hole.

The low-tension contact maker (of the battery ignition) is very rarely found to be out of order, but the following

Battery Ignition. examinations can be made. Having satisfied yourself that the platinum points (Fig. 159) are clean, flat and true, and that the blade is tightened so that the platinum pointed screw is opposite the platinum on the blade and that the blade has sufficient set upon it to push the platinum points into firm contact when the screw is correctly advanced, proceed to set the contacts in the following manner :—Remove the high-tension distributor, and take off the side cover (as shown on page 159), then turn the engine round until the roller on the little actuating lever is on the lowest portion of the cam, that is to say, on the middle of one of the flat portions of the cam. Then with the platinum points screwed well apart, proceed to advance the platinum screw slowly (Fig. 160) until the trembler of the induction coil indicates that the platinum screw has just come into contact with the platinum on the blade, then give the screw *a further half turn* and check up the small screw on the side which secures it. If this is correctly done the trembler will be found to work during periods amounting to a total of one-third of a revolution of the commutator, and remain stationary during a total of two-thirds ; if it fails to do so, some mistake has arisen and the platinum screw should be re-adjusted until it does so.

If, however, the trembler is kept lightly set and in good order, this low-tension contact ought not to require any attention for a whole season.

When replacing the wires on to the distributor, see that the number cut on the ebonite of each terminal corresponds with the figure marked at each hole.

TREMBLER OF COIL.
(Fig. 161, page 139.)

The following is the proper method of adjusting the trembler of the induction coil (box on dashboard) :—

Having seen that the platinum points are in really first-class condition—sound, flat, clean and true—proceed to test whether the iron armature has sufficient " set " on the spring to just lift it away from the core of the coil. The amount of force should not be more than 3 or 4 grammes or $\frac{1}{10}$th oz., which is about the weight of a lead pencil of half its maximum length. This armature should also have free play

of about $\frac{1}{16}$ in. between its touching the end of the core and falling back against its stop. As this part is generally arranged by the makers, unless the coil has worn to some

FIG. 159.
LOW-TENSION CONTACT BREAKER.

FIG. 160.
ADJUSTING CONTACT BREAKER.

extent or had very rough handling, it should not be necessary to make any alteration to this part.

In addition to the iron armature, there is the spring plate which carries the platinum point, to be put in place and screwed down, taking care that the two platinum points are opposite one another. This spring should have a slight upward curvature sufficient to cause the platinum points to make contact with a pressure of about ½ oz. or 15 grammes. Should this pressure be too great a large amount of current will be taken by the coil and the platinum points will not last well. If, however, it is too slack, it may fail to make contact sufficiently quickly when the engine is running at a fast speed.

It is the upward pressure of this spring which is the most difficult part of the adjustment to make, it being a simple matter after this is correct to follow our usual instructions as follows :—

To adjust the platinum point, start with the points quite apart, turn on the battery current, screw down the screw slowly until the action of the trembler shows that the points have just come into contact, then give the screw a further quarter of a turn which will ensure good contact and the correct amount of *play* for the iron armature, *viz.*, $\frac{1}{100}$ of an inch.

If the trembler is set with too much weight on the platinum points the coil will take an excess of current, causing not only the burning of the platinum points on the trembler but also those on the low-tension commutator.

MAGNETO FAILING AT LOW SPEEDS.

If the magneto failed to effect proper ignition at slow speeds of the engine, it would probably be due to :—

(a) The points on the sparking plugs being too far apart.

(b) The platinum contact on the magneto having burnt itself out of adjustment, and therefore not making contact for the right length of time.

(c) The magnetism of the magneto becoming weak (demagnetisation) ; this might be after three or four years' use. Test with screw-driver.

IGNITION NOTES.

Test battery ignition upon coming to a stopping place to see that it is in good order and capable of firing all cylinders.

See that plates of batteries are not buckled or blistered, battery case clean, acid clear, of right density and sufficient to cover the plates. Battery terminals may be greased to prevent corrosion.

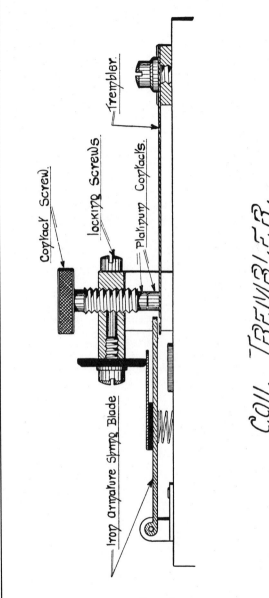

FIG. 161.

Keep magneto ignition well advanced but always in the position where the engine seems *most powerful* when the throttle is opened, because that is the best position for the speed at which the engine was running when throttle was opened.

A weak mixture or a throttled-down mixture should be ignited earlier than a full charge of the full strength.

Remember to lubricate the magneto at the various points (see "Lubrication").

Keep wires free from oil.

Wires leading to plugs should not be "bunched" but separated as much as possible.

If the coil box is much exposed to rain and wet it should have a waterproof cover fitted.

Dirt and dust should be kept out of the coil box, and the ebonite and fittings should be carefully dusted occasionally (without upsetting the trembler adjustment).

In case of trembler troubles, the "earth" connections should be inspected to see if sound.

To prevent undue "pitting" of the platinum points, the direction of current should be reversed, by changing over the battery terminals, about every 1,000 miles, or each time the accumulators are being fitted after re-charging.

Special sparking plugs should be used for the magneto ignition, which are different to those used for the battery ignition. Plugs of the "Pognon" make intended for the magneto ignition are marked "M." (NOTE.—Magneto plugs may be used for the battery ignition but not *vice versa*.)

It should be noted that the battery plugs should be situated over the inlet valves, and the magneto plugs over the exhaust valves ; we have sometimes noticed clients' cars on which these have been changed over in error.

A special descriptive pamphlet dealing with the Bosch Magneto System can be obtained on request.

APPENDIX IX.

CARBURATION.

The ROLLS-ROYCE Duplex Carburettor is made with two jets, with their corresponding air passages. When the engine is running slowly, throttled down, only one jet (the right-hand smaller one) is open, and as the throttle is opened the second one automatically comes into action, and as the engine increases in speed the automatic supplementary air valve (Fig. 162) admits additional air. The whole arrangement is so constructed as to insure sufficiently

FIG. 162.
LIFTING AIR VALVE.

vigorous suction at slow speeds and perfectly free passage of the gases at high speeds, and, at the same time, to keep the ratio between air and spirit constant.

The engine is not only more economical but it also works more satisfactorily when the quantity of spirit is the smallest possible amount that will ignite promptly. The engine should therefore be run with the weakest possible mixture, and owing to the fact that the atmospheric conditions and motor spirits vary, we provide means of adjusting the quantity of spirit (through a certain range) from the dashboard. This also enables the driver to test whether the carburation is correct.

Should it be found necessary, however, to dismantle the whole carburettor, the readjustment can be made quite easily by taking care that the small levers are clamped upon the regulating nuts when the screws are exactly level with the top of the nuts, and the marks on the nuts parallel as in Fig. 163, with the dashboard regulator in the central position. Fig. 163 shows the correct markings on the jet screws, when the dashboard regulator is in middle position. If, however, some part has been broken or replaced so as to render useless this indication of the manufacturer's setting, then proceed as follows: Put the dashboard regulator in the central position and slack off the levers which are clamped to the milled nuts, screw the milled nuts round so that the cones controlled by these milled nuts just open the

FIG. 163.

petrol spray, then make an attempt to start the engine by "flooding" or putting a small quantity of petrol in the induction pipe, or both. As soon as you are able to get the engine to fire, make a rough adjustment as quickly as possible, so as to keep the engine running. Now throttle the engine down by putting the governor lever as low as possible, and proceed to regulate the slow speed jet (right-hand one) until the engine runs steadily with the smallest amount of petrol, which means that the nut is screwed as far as possible in a right-handed direction (clockwise, looking at the top). In reducing this low speed jet to the minimum, the engine may commence to "hunt" on the governor, which is an

indication that the jet has been reduced too much. It should then slowly be increased by turning anti-clockwise until the engine runs steadily when warm with the smallest amount of petrol and at a reasonably slow speed. The bolt on the lever can then be tightened.

Then proceed to adjust the high speed jet as follows: Advance the ignition half-way up the quadrant, using both battery and magneto ignition, open the throttle wide by hand, and while the engine is running very fast with the throttle wide open, screw the milled nut clockwise until the engine shows definite signs of dropping in speed through getting insufficient petrol to ignite quickly.

Now proceed to tighten the bolt which clamps the lever on to the screw, and the car should then be taken on the

FIG. 164.
UNSCREWING AIR VALVE CAP.

road and the hand lever can be tried in various positions to test if the carburation can be made too weak by putting the lever in its extreme weak position, and if it cannot be made too weak to run at its fastest speed, then the high speed jet can be reduced (say quarter of a turn at a time) until, upon testing, it is found that the hand regulator will effectively reduce the petrol to below the minimum for best running.

It will be noticed that this puts into the hands of the driver the power to have the correct mixture at high or low speeds and if it is found that the engine fails to run economically or misses fire at high or low speeds, the jet can be separately regulated so as to correct any such fault

A point to remember is to keep the air valve (Fig. 162), clean by taking it to pieces occasionally and rubbing it with a clean cloth, free from fluff, at the same time avoiding any form of lubrication whatever. It is got at by unscrewing two screws (Fig. 164) and taking off the cap with spring attached (Fig. 165).

The air valve should be drawn out slowly and carefully, so as not to distort same or bend centre spindle.

The diaphragm should be square and firmly attached to air valve, be flush with top of throat, i.e., should open throat as soon as lifted, and should cut off throat when down.

The air valve should be sluggish without sticking ('005" clearance); it should take about three seconds to close itself

FIG. 165.
AIR VALVE CAP REMOVED.

when pushed in close. The spring should just touch the air valve when down. The cone valves to petrol sprays should not stick but respond to hand control. The air valve should be down at very low engine speeds, commence to rise as soon as accelerated and lift to the top at high speeds (about 1,500 revs.).

There should be an air-tight joint to cover of air chamber (top side).

The float chamber should occasionally be opened up (Figs. 166 and 167), and the bottom cleaned out; examine the float (Fig. 167) to see that it is air-tight and contains no petrol inside it.

THROTTLE VALVE.

With reference to the throttle valve, this should be capable of being completely closed by the governor after the engine has been raced with the foot accelerator. If

FIG. 166.
FLOAT CHAMBER COVER REMOVED.

FIG. 167.
FLOAT AND NEEDLE VALVE.

this is not the case, the control of the engine is apt to be faulty at slow speeds. Also, if the throttle valve gets worn and is so slack as to allow the engine to draw any gas when it should be shut, firing in the silencer may occur after running downhill or upon closing the throttle after a fast run.

CONSUMPTION.

On dry, level roads a gallon of petrol should carry a car of average weight with an average load about 15 miles; if the consumption is much inferior to this the following points should be looked to :—The carburettor may give too rich a mixture and the jets may be reduced by the hand lever on dashboard; the timing of the ignition may be incorrect or the car may have been driven with the ignition lever too much retarded; the automatic air valve or piston in the carburettor may not be working freely; the float or needle valve may not be working freely, causing

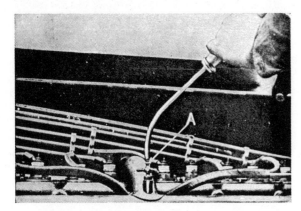

FIG. 168.
COCK A IN INDUCTION PIPE.

"flooding"; there may be a leak of air in one of the inlet pipes between the carburettor and cylinders; or there may be a leakage of petrol at the bottom of the tank, or along the petrol feed pipe or at the filter, or at one of the unions of the petrol supply.

MISSING FIRE.

If this should occur and it is not traceable to any fault in the ignitions, there may be other causes :—

If the mixture is not properly adjusted, the engine may refuse to run on all the cylinders. Missing-fire may there-

fore occur through faulty adjustment of the carburettor (*q.v.*, p. 142), or when the piston (Fig. 162 p. 141) of the automatic air-valve has stuck.

Missing-fire may also occur owing to the sticking of exhaust valves. This can be often remedied by pouring a little paraffin on to the top of the exhaust valve.

If at any time it should be found that, when the car has run a short distance with the throttle wide open, "firing" takes place in the carburettor, and there are other signs of petrol "starvation," it would be as well to carefully clean out all the petrol pipes and connections, as these are liable to become coated as time goes on.

If the engine will not run well at slow speeds, look to the induction pipe. This should be sound, and there should be no external leak between the throttle **Missing at** and the cylinders. This is best tested **Low Speeds.** by closing the throttle and blowing through the small cock A on the induction pipe (Fig. 168). The pipes, etc., should be capable of being filled without leaking. It is disastrous to the slow running of the engine if any air is drawn into the cylinders otherwise than through the carburettor. The small cock should always be closed when running.

"Misfires" may be caused by faulty compression (see under "Compression").